A Handbook of
Social Science Research

A Handbook of Social Science Research

Beverly R. Dixon
Gary D. Bouma
G. B. J. Atkinson

OXFORD UNIVERSITY PRESS

Oxford University Press, Walton Street, Oxford OX2 6DP

Oxford New York Toronto
Delhi Bombay Calcutta Madras Karachi
Petaling Jaya Singapore Hong Kong Tokyo
Nairobi Dar es Salaam Cape Town
Melbourne Auckland
and associated companies in
Berlin Ibadan

Oxford is a trade mark of Oxford University Press

Published in the United States
by Oxford University Press, New York

First published 1987 in hardback and paperback
Paperback reprinted 1988, 1990, 1991, 1992

British Library Cataloguing in Publication Data
Dixon, Beverly R.
Handbook of social sciences research.
[British ed.]
1. Social sciences—Methodology   I. Title   II. Bouma, Gary D.
III. Atkinson, G. B. J.   IV. Dixon, Beverly R. Research process
300'.72   H61
ISBN 0–19–878023–0

Library of Congress Cataloging in Publication Data
Dixon, Beverly R.
Handbook of social science research.
Rev. ed.: The research process/Beverly R. Dixon,
Gary D. Bouma. 1984.
Includes index.
1. Social sciences—Research.   I. Bouma, Gary D.   II. Atkinson, G. B. J.
III. Dixon, Beverly, R. Research process.   IV. Title.
H62.D583 1987   300'.72   86–23533
ISBN 0–19–878023–0

Printed and bound in Great Britain by
Biddles Ltd, Guildford and King's Lynn

To Donald H. Bouma
and Dorothy Mary Atkinson

Acknowledgements

This is the British edition of *The Research Process*, a successful Australian book. In the original edition the authors, Beverly Dixon and Gary Bouma, paid tribute to the help they received from their colleagues and students. Similarly in editing the British edition I have drawn on ideas given to me by colleagues, including my wife, and would like to thank them for their help.

The authors and publishers wish to thank the following copyright holders for permission to reproduce material in this book: pp. 8–9 *The Sunday Times*; pp. 30–1 *The Guardian*; pp. 156–8 *The Journal of Educational Psychology* and *Educational Research*; pp. 164–6 *British Psychological Society*; p. 194 *The Financial Times*.

Brian Atkinson
Lancashire Polytechnic, Preston

Contents

To the teacher

A Handbook of Social Science Research is a resource text for students and teachers. It is aimed at college and university students taking introductory research methods courses or undertaking small scale research projects. Students taking GCE A level or equivalent courses should also find it useful.

The text assumes little entry knowledge about research processes. Hence the text begins in a rather leisurely way, introducing concepts one at a time and providing clarifying examples at each critical juncture. Further, the book takes a non-statistical, non-mathematical approach, thereby presenting the essentials of the research process in what may, to many students, be a more understandable manner.

The text approaches research methodology as a *process*. A sequence of learnable activities is presented. Each activity prepares the novice researcher for the next step. Some questions are best answered before others when doing social science research. Reasons for the sequencing are explained to the reader and pitfalls are flagged.

Several examples are developed in detail and carried through each chapter of the text in order to help the student to see how the research process progresses. In addition, there are exercises and questions throughout the text which help the student to learn by practising what has just been discussed. Each chapter ends with questions to help students check their comprehension of the material presented.

There are two dangerous extremes to avoid in teaching students how to do research. The first is to give the impression that there is no pattern to the process at all. The second is to insist that students slavishly follow one or other approach. Students are often so eager to collect data that they ignore the essential first steps. More than anything else, doing research requires clear and disciplined thinking.

A Handbook of Social Science Research is designed to develop the research skills which are important for living and working in our world—a world in which information is becoming one of the most valuable commodities and in which the ability to handle information is one of the most valuable and marketable skills.

To the student

Social science research—what is it? How do you do it? When do you do it? What are the pitfalls? What are the 'tricks of the trade'? *A Handbook of Social Science Research* has the answers.

The *Handbook* assumes that you have little more than a vague idea of what social science research is. It does *not* assume that you are a mathematical whiz-kid capable of doing chi squares or standard deviations in your sleep. In fact, the book requires that, mathematically, you be capable of little more than calculating a mean.

This text guides you step by step through the process of social science research. Chapter 1 talks about 'How we know what we know' and suggests that research is a means of checking what we think we know.

This text is directive about the ordering of the steps in the research process. It warns of the pitfalls of rushing off to collect data before you are very clear about what it is you want to study. The text divides the process of social science research into phases, phases which must be done in sequential order. Phase 1 involves:

1 selecting a problem (including narrowing and clarifying the problem, and stating the problem as a hypothesis or research objective);
2 defining variables and determining ways of measuring them;
3 choosing a research design and
4 organizing a sample.

Phase 2 is the data collection stage. Here we have included some comments about how to be an ethical researcher and a wise one! Phase 3, of course, is the phase in which you find out what your data tells you. Here you analyse and interpret your findings and draw conclusions.

Research can be fun. But this is only true if you keep yourself organized and follow through the process in logical order. We hope that this book will go a long way in making your entrance into the world of social science research both competent and enjoyable.

Introduction

1

How we know what we know and how we know we know

Answering our questions
Consulting an authority as a way of knowing
Research as a way of knowing
Questions for review

Have you ever had an argument with someone? She said one thing and you said another. She claimed she was right because she read it in a book. You argued that a doctor told you, and a doctor should know, after all. So arguments go. But how do they stop? How do you win an argument? How do you know when you are right, or wrong? How do we know what we know?

We are confronted by questions all through our lives. What is the best diet to help me lose weight? Will my parents' marriage break up if my father loses his job? What is the best way to prepare for an examination? What do teenagers really want? Are people lazier today? Is tertiary education worth while? Hundreds of questions—some big, others small; some crucial, others trivial—pop up as we live. Each question could easily be the start of an argument or a long debate. How do we answer our questions?

Answering our questions

We answer our questions in a variety of ways. If we want to know whether it is raining we can look outside ourselves or ask someone. We can answer the questions ourselves or take someone's word for it. Some questions can be answered quickly with a look out of the window, or in the right cupboard. Where is my notebook? Is Fred here yet? Other questions are more

3

complex. But the choice is roughly the same. We can answer the question ourselves or take someone's word for it. We can either do the research ourselves or consult an authority.

Consulting an authority as a way of knowing

The most common way in which we answer our questions is to consult an authority. We ask someone who knows. If we have a question, we look up the answer in an encyclopaedia, we ask a friend who knows, we call the doctor, we ask our teacher, or religious leader, or the principal, or the police, or the umpire. We are used to asking authorities. We refer to articles in journals or the newspaper, or look for a book on the subject in the library or bookshop.

A friend of ours thought he had the world on a string. He had been given a very large, very comprehensive, one-volume, 3,000-page encyclopaedia with special sections on geology, human anatomy, medicine, and the planets. He was confident that the answers to all the questions he might ever ask would be found in that authority. Imagine his disappointment when he discovered a question to which the encyclopaedia provided an inadequate answer. We are always disappointed when our authorities fail us.

So long as the authority consulted does in fact know the answer, it is most efficient to refer our questions to an authority. The problem with consulting authority is a problem of selection. On what bases do we choose our authorities? The only real basis should be that the authority has the knowledge we need. Does the authority know what we want to know? If we plan to consult an authority in order to answer a question, we want to be sure that the authority is knowledgeable about that subject. That is where one of the problems of consulting authorities arises. While knowledge should be the criterion for choosing an authority, there are often other reasons. How does someone come to be seen as an authority?

Popularity or the possession of a particular talent seem to convey authority. Athletes are asked to promote products as diverse as razor blades and milk. Why is it that we pay more attention to Steve Cramm or Bryan Robson than to the person next door? Advertising relies heavily on the fact that we will pay attention to heroes and superstars. Do you know that tall people are seen as more authoritative than short ones? It's a fact: that is, research has demonstrated that it is true. Do you know that well-dressed people are seen as more authoritative than shabbily-dressed people? It's a fact. To people raised in a western culture at this time, someone in a lab coat is seen to be particularly authoritative. It has not always been this way. In the past, parsons, country squires, or other community leaders were seen as authorities. The point is that certain

---

Test yourself

Who would you be more likely to believe? Who is more of an authority for you? in the columns below the pictures place one of these symbols:

B = You would tend to believe this person's word in this area.
D = You would tend to doubt this person's word in this area.
NR = not relevant.

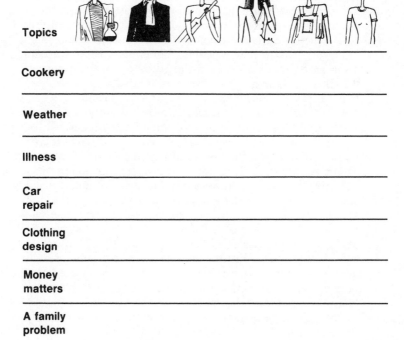

Topics

Cookery

Weather

Illness

Car repair

Clothing design

Money matters

A family problem

Discuss your assessment of these 'authorities' with your friends. What clues are contained in each picture about the person's area of authority? What did you assume about the person in the lab coat? Would you have made different assumptions if that person were male or female? Old or young? Black or Asian? There are many reasons why we think people are authorities. Let us look at some of them.

characteristics—age, gender, class, clothing, height, tone of voice, accent—tend to influence whether we see people as authoritative. Characteristics which may have nothing to do with how much people know about a subject still affect our choice of the people we consider to be authorities.

Another way people come to be seen as authorities is by the positions they hold. In this case the person has authority because of position, rather than by virtue of knowledge or any other attribute. The police have authority to order you to stop, to leave your car, to answer certain questions. They have this authority because of their position, because they are police. Parents have authority over children. Judges have authority to pass sentence on law breakers. Priests, ministers, and rabbis have authority to marry people. Sometimes people who are given authority to do certain things are taken to be authorities on other subjects as well.

It can be confusing when someone who has authority in one area is taken to be, or presumes to be, an authority in others. In the past this could be quite troublesome. Monarchs, by virtue of their power to imprison, tax, or kill, could make their opinion binding on the people; disagreement could bring death. Today we are unlikely to take the monarch's opinion on, let us say, nutrition to be authoritative. Persons with authority are seen to have *limited* authority. If we were having an argument about what is the best way to prepare for an examination we would probably not consult any of the authorities listed above—police, priests, parents, or monarchs. If we were to consult a teacher, someone who has a certain amount of authority to do certain things, we would be asking the teacher because we assumed that the teacher might know more about taking exams than other people.

The critical point here is that no matter how prominent the person, no matter how much authority and power someone may have on account of position, the opinion of that person on a subject in which they are not expert is of no more value than the opinion of any other person. A bishop may hold opinions about unemployment, taxation, the way we raise families, the role of the government in foreign aid. These opinions, unless grounded in special knowledge relevant to each of the above areas, are of no more consequence than those expressed on the same topics by anyone else. Similarly, a professor of botany may have an opinion on which diet is better for you but is unlikely to have special knowledge making her expert in the field of nutrition. The fact that the opinion is expressed by a 'professor' should give it no added weight unless it is in the professor's field.

We can now see that people can have at least two kinds of authority: authority due to position and authority due to knowledge. The kind of authority we are usually looking for is authority due to knowledge. While we may call on the police to stop an argument which has become violent, we do not ask police to settle the issue.

We call on an authority to settle our arguments and answer our questions when we have reason to believe that the authority may know something about the issue. We consult a doctor to find out what is making us feel unwell or in pain. We trust that the doctor has more knowledge of the workings of our bodies than we do. The physician is an authority because of special knowledge in a given field.

But we have problems here too. Authority due to knowledge is limited to the field of that knowledge. It is unfortunate that some people who have authority to speak in one field act as though they have authority to speak in any field. It is always important to ask, 'In what is this person an authority?' Members of the medical profession are sometimes asked to be authorities on all subjects. While expert in the functioning and repair of the human body, doctors are not usually especially well informed on social problems. Does being an authority in medicine make one an authority on disarmament? No. Or you might ask, of what relevance is being a physicist to making pronouncements about the nutritional value of chocolate bars?

Research as a way of knowing

Inevitably, the ultimate problem with consulting authorities will arise. Two recognized authorities in the same field will disagree.

Or the person with whom we are arguing will not accept the authority we chose to consult. Or someone will ask a question the authorities cannot answer. Like our friend's encyclopaedia, authorities are limited. What do we do then? We conduct research. When we want to know something and there is no authority, or the authorities disagree, or we just are not ready to accept without question what the authority has told us, then we do research. When the existing literature on a subject does not answer the question we are asking, or we are dissatisfied with the answer, then we do research.

How do we know? We either know it ourself, because of our experiences, our research, or we know it because we have chosen to accept the word of some authority. There is nothing wrong with accepting the authority of others. We would be in a sorry state if we insisted on learning everything by our own direct experience. However, the word of authorities should be accepted critically and authorities should be chosen carefully.

One way to improve our ability to select authorities and to evaluate what they say is to learn how to do research. If we are familiar with the requirements of sound research we can evaluate the statements of experts more easily; we can ask better questions. Hence one more reason for learning about the research process stems from our need to evaluate the statements of authorities. How do they know that? What kind of research lies behind that claim? Have they considered . . . ?

You have questions. Organizations and groups have questions too. Organizations and groups engage in research when they need answers to questions. Read the following extract from an article in the *Sunday Times*. Why are they researching?

If a woman is one of the 0.5% in whom breast cancer is detected by mammography in Edinburgh, she goes to the breast unit in Longmore hospital to meet a friendly team of doctors, radiologists, and nurses, who will give her information about different treatments. Professor Forrest says: 'We have tried to establish an excellent service for patients, but we are also trying to advance our knowledge of the disease.'

All the women who go to Longmore receive letters explaining that several controlled studies, in which treatments vary, are being carried out and asking them to participate. These trials, many of them financed by public donations through bodies such as the Cancer Research Campaign, are going on all over the country to compare:

- Lumpectomy (removal only of the lump) to mastectomy (removal of the entire breast)
- Lumpectomy with radiotherapy to lumpectomy without
- Surgery with tamoxifen (an anti-oestrogen drug) to surgery alone in younger and older women
- Surgery with chemotherapy to surgery alone in younger women
- Chemotherapy to removing the ovaries in young women with fast-moving disease.

The latest results from studies in America and Italy suggest that women with early breast cancer treated by lumpectomy and radiotherapy (to control local spread of the disease) do at least as well as those who undergo disfiguring mastectomy. As a result, some British specialists are making every effort to conserve breasts where possible. In Edinburgh, Professor Forrest says, 'screening swings the pendulum over to less extreme treatment. The number of mastectomies we perform now is relatively small—maybe one to every four lumpectomies.' Other doctors are more cautious. Alan McKinna, consultant surgeon at the Royal Marsden in London, says. 'I think it's important to treat the whole person and tell her that mastectomy is still the yardstick— the least number of local recurrences follow major surgery. But where possible I carry out an operation which removes the tumour and conserves the breast.'

Lumpectomy removes the primary tumour. However, breast cancer is often a systemic disease (one which can spread to other parts of the body) so in many cases another form of treatment is necessary to prevent the spread of cancer in the breast area and to other organs.

The most hopeful recent advances in systemic treatment came from a summit meeting in London last November where world specialists met to compare the interim results of 40 trials carried out on some tens of thousands of women who have been treated by either mastectomy or lumpectomy.

The preliminary review of these trials indicated that anti-cancer drugs (chemotherapy) increased the survival rate of women under 50 by over a third in the first few years after surgery. Hormone treatment with tamoxifen can increase the survival of women over 50 by 20% over the same trial period.

The Sunday Times, 28 July 1985

In this case the reason for the research is very clear; they hope to save lives. In order to establish the best method of treatment they have to engage in a great deal of carefully executed research. If the result of their work is clear cut, they will be able to decide the best treatment, not by guessing or by an appeal to authority, but by an appeal to the evidence. Research is done to find out. What is happening? How does it work? Which produces better results? Which statement is true?

When we want to know something and we are not satisfied with the word of authorities, we do research. When we are faced with a question to which there is no answer at present, or to which the authorities give conflicting or unsatisfactory answers, we do research. Research is a disciplined way of coming to know something about ourselves or our world. Research is a process for answering some of the questions we ask, for settling disputes over the correct answer to our questions.

Questions for review

1 What are two ways of knowing or answering questions?
2 Two kinds of authority have been mentioned in this chapter. What are they? Define each. Give an example of each.
3 Discuss some of the problems involved in consulting authorities to answer our questions. For example, try to find:
   ● an authority on bringing up children
   ● an authority on dry cleaning
   ● an authority on what to wear to a dance
   ● an authority on cricket
   On what basis did you select your authority?
4 As a class, or with some friends, make a list of authorities you regularly rely on.
   Discuss whether it is possible to live without accepting the word of authorities.
5 List five reasons why people do research.

2

Research as a way of knowing

Research as a process
Research as a discipline
Theory and data
Questions for review

Those who claim that their remedy works, or is better, or no worse than some other remedy are usually asked to show the evidence for their claim. Similarly, those who claim that a particular diet is more healthy should show the evidence in support of their claim. Those who argue that a particular programme of driver education will reduce the number of road accidents are asked to present their evidence. We engage in research to settle conflicting claims or differences of opinion, or to test an idea. Take the following simple case.

Mary: The fastest way to drive from Preston to Leeds is to use the motorway.

Frank: No way! It's much further than the direct route and there are likely to be delays because of motorway repairs.

The conflict between Mary and Frank can be settled by research. They both have 'theories' about the fastest way to drive from Preston to Leeds. We suspect that you could probably design a piece of research to test these theories. Research is the disciplined way we come to know what we know. Research is one way of knowing.

Research as a process

To do research is to be involved in a process. A process can be seen as a series of linked activities moving from a beginning to

11

an end. The research process is not a rigid process. A rigid process is one in which Step A must be done and completed before Step B can begin. On the other hand, there is a sense in which, if the first steps are not executed carefully, the rest of the research process will be weakened or made more difficult.

Those who have done a lot of research develop their own style of going through the phases of the research process. Each researcher will be able to describe a pattern, a reasonably regular way in which she goes about doing research. It can be said that there is a 'normal' sequence in the research process.

By 'normal' we do not mean to indicate a rigid, dogmatic, 'this, then that' ordering. Rather, there is an order of basic stages and a series of interlinked issues in each stage.

We have chosen a particular way of describing the research process because it seems to us to help students to learn the necessary skills and, if followed, to prevent many of the major pitfalls in research. We do not see this way as the only way, just one useful way.

The research process can be outlined as follows:

Outline of the research process

Phase 1: essential first steps
During Phase 1 the researcher clarifies the issue to be researched and selects a research method.

Phase 2: data collection
During Phase 2 the researcher collects evidence about the research question.

Phase 3: analysis and interpretation
During this phase the researcher relates the evidence collected to the research question asked, draws conclusions about the question, and acknowledges the limitations of the research.

In order to provide a sense of the flow of the whole process we will go through each phase and describe the major activities in each. We will develop a small piece of research as we go through the phases as an example.

Phase 1: essential first steps
1 Selecting, narrowing, and formulating the problem to be studied.
2 Selecting a research design.
3 Designing and devising measures for variables.
4 Setting up tables for analysis.
5 Selecting a sample.

Phase 1 of the research process involves five essential first steps. These steps are essential because failure to address these issues satisfactorily will undermine, or make more difficult, the rest of the research process. A question that is unclear or too broad cannot be answered. Research is conducted according to a plan or design. Without clear definitions confusion results. If you know how you are going to analyse your data, you are clearer about what data you really need. A decision about a sample is made before data are collected. These are the things which need to be done first if the research is to be conducted successfully.

Remember the argument between Mary and Frank about which route between Preston and Leeds was faster? Both Frank and Mary had a hunch, or a 'theory' about which route was faster. We will devise a piece of research to test their theories. What must be done in Phase 1?

First, we need to focus the question:
1 Are normal or special cars to be used?
2 Are cars to be driven by normal or specially trained drivers?
3 Are speed limits to be observed? One route may be faster only if the speed limit is exceeded.
4 At what time of the day, on which day of the week do we want to do this?
5 Will we be satisfied with a single test or will more than one be required? How many?
6 Will any other routes be considered?
7 Will any allowances be made for time lost due to accident, breakdown, or road hazard (like a stone through the windscreen)?

There are doubtless other questions that would have to be asked if we were to do this seriously. But let us say that we decided to run the test on one Friday afternoon in May with

two equally matched drivers and cars starting at Preston Town
Hall with instructions to keep all road safety laws. The first car
to arrive at Leeds Town Hall will be declared to have taken the
faster route.
Now the first part of this little piece of research has been
completed. The research question has been clarified and
narrowed. It is no longer what is the faster route from Preston
to Leeds, but which is the faster route from Preston Town Hall
to Leeds Town Hall on a specific Friday afternoon in May. The
variables have been defined and measured. Car A or Car B will
arrive first. Car A will have gone via the motorway. Car B will
have gone via ordinary roads. The variable is which car arrives
first, A or B. For the first test a single run is acceptable.
Now that all this has been clarified, it is possible to move on
to the next phase in the research process, Phase 2: data
collection.

Phase 2: data collection
1 Collecting data.
2 Summarizing and organizing data.

While many have the impression that data collection is
the major enterprise in research, this is not strictly correct.
Preparation, Phase 1, takes the most time, and drawing
conclusions and writing the report takes more time than
data collection in most cases. Data collection itself takes the
least time. You will learn this for yourself as you engage in
research.
Returning to our homely example, we can see that collecting
data for this research involves two cars driving from the town
hall in Preston to the town hall in Leeds on a given Friday
afternoon in May. The data to be collected will be that either
Car A arrived first or Car B arrived first, or that they arrived
together. Such data pose no problems of summarization or of
organization.
Once data have been collected and organized you are ready
for the last phase of research, Phase 3.
In Phase 3 you relate the data collected to the research
question and draw conclusions. It is really quite simple, if you
can keep the research problem under control.

Phase 3: analysis and interpretation
1 Relating data to the research question.
2 Drawing conclusions.
3 Assessing the limitations of the study.
4 Making suggestions for further research.

For the sake of continuing our example, let us say that Car A arrived in Leeds a full thirty minutes before Car B. What would you conclude? Whose theory would have a piece of data supporting it, Mary's or Frank's? Whose theory would be seriously questioned as a result of the evidence produced by this bit of research?

You may be able to see some limitations or shortcomings to our study. It applies only to one Friday in May under certain conditions. Only one trial was made. The outcome might have been the result of an accident which held up traffic for three-quarters of an hour. Different drivers, or cars, or days might produce different results.

Think of some other limitations which should be included in the research report. Propose another piece of research which would answer some of the questions that remain after the bit of research just done. For example, the same trial could be done on different days, or more often.

We hope that you can begin to see that research is a process by which our questions are sharpened or focused; a process by which data are gathered in such a way that we can begin to answer the questions we asked. You can probably also see how having completed one piece of research, you are usually led to more questions and more research. This is another way in which research is a continuous process. The end of one project is often the beginning of the next.

Research as a discipline

Research requires discipline. Research is a disciplined way to go about answering questions. This distinguishes research from other ways of answering questions. The fact that research is a disciplined process means that the answers are more reliable.

Asking the right questions

The first and probably the hardest discipline required by the research process is to learn to ask the right questions. The problems that motivate us to do research are often enormous. How to prevent nuclear war? How to save the economy? How to prevent cot death? How to improve the quality of life for all people? The first discipline is to move from these 'global' questions to researchable questions.

Researchable questions have two basic properties. First, they are limited in scope to certain times, places, and conditions. A researchable question is usually a small fragment of a larger question. One of the hardest things for a researcher to do is to leave behind that larger burning issue and settle down to tackle one small, manageable part of it. To fail to do so, of course, would mean that the work was doomed because the problem addressed would be larger than the time, energy, or other resources available. It is better to answer a small question than to leave a large one unanswered. Perhaps by piecing together a number of smaller answers a large answer may be discovered.

For example, the question: 'What factors affect family decision-making?' is a very large question. A more manageable question would be: 'Does knowledge of nutrition play a role in the decisions made about what to serve for tea in a particular family or small group of families?' Similarly, in order to be researched, the question: 'Does adequate nutrition promote academic performance?' would have to be focused, narrowed, and limited.

The best and probably the only way to learn the skill of narrowing and focusing a broad issue so that it becomes a research question is to practise.

Try your hand at limiting the question: 'Does nutrition play a role in sports performance?'

In order to help you get started, let us look at the question. As it stands it looks like a simple question requiring a yes or no answer. To become a research question, it needs to be more specific. It helps to ask a few basic questions:

What are the main things, ideas or activities in the question? Nutrition and Sports Performance

The question asks something about the relationship between nutrition and sports performance. Once you identify the main elements you can ask another question.

What about nutrition?

Well, that refers to what people eat. How much? How often? What kinds of food? One way of making this question more specific is to narrow it down.

How much is eaten?
How often is food eaten?
What kinds of food are eaten?
Does the kind of food eaten affect sports performance?

While more specific, the question is not as specific as it could be. Can you narrow it further?

How much and what kind of protein?
How do vegetarian diets compare?
What about the amount of carbohydrate?

Part of the question has been narrowed. Now there is the other part—sports performance. How can you make that more specific?

What about sports performance?
Are you comparing who wins?
Are you testing for endurance?
Are you measuring stamina?
What sport?

You might narrow this to tennis. Your research question might be:

Will players who have eaten some carbohydrate within half an hour of playing perform better at tennis (that is, win) than players who have eaten nothing within the three hours before playing?

Now try your hand at limiting these questions:

1 What factors are important in family decision-making?

Hints: Try listing some factors, for example, economic.
Limit the area of decision-making.

2 Can we promote the development of a positive self-image among handicapped teenagers?

Hints: What do you know about self-image?
What are key factors which lead to a healthy self-
image, or to a negative self-image?

The first property of a research question is that it is limited
in scope, narrowed in focus, and confined to a certain time,
place, and set of conditions. While frustrating and difficult, the
discipline required to focus the research question is one of the
most important in the research process.

The second property of a researchable question is that
some observable, tangible, countable evidence or data can
be gathered which is relevant to the question. Research can
deal only with the observable, measurable aspects of the
questions we might want to have answered. This is very
frustrating to some people. For example, questions of morality
are not answerable by the kind of research we are talking
about. Research cannot determine whether an action is right or
wrong. The question 'Is it right to allow terminally ill patients
to die?' is not answerable by empirical research. Empirical
research is that kind of research which seeks to answer those
questions which can be answered by reference to sensory data.
Sensory data are data that can be seen, touched, measured,
counted.

---

empirical   Based on, or guided by, the results of observation and
experiment only. From the Greek word *empeirikós* meaning
experienced, skilled.

Shorter Oxford English Dictionary

While empirical research cannot answer the moral question 'Is
it right or wrong to allow terminally ill patients to die?', it can
answer the question 'How many students in a particular home
economics class think that it is right or wrong to allow certain
types of terminally ill patients to die?' One of the disciplines
associated with doing research is to learn to ask questions which
have measurable, sensory, countable answers. That is, questions
which can be answered in terms of observations.

There are other kinds of questions to which there are not
empirical answers. For example, questions of beauty. Is the
Taj Mahal more or less beautiful than Cologne Cathedral? Are

the Highlands of Scotland more beautiful than Cornwall? Is the Tower of London more beautiful than Edinburgh Castle? These questions comparing the beauty of things are questions of aesthetics not empirical questions. Of course, they could be turned into empirical questions.

Make up an empirical question relating to one of the aesthetic questions above. For example, 'How many London University students of architecture consider this picture of Cologne Cathedral to be more beautiful than this picture of the Taj Mahal?'

These same issues can be raised about questions of taste, fashion, etiquette, morality, religion, and political ideology. Empirical research cannot determine which table setting is most tasteful, or which jacket is most fashionable. These are not empirical questions. Research could answer such questions as which table setting is judged to be most tasteful by home economics students in a particular college, or a sample of housewives, or interior decorators. Empirical research cannot determine questions of religious faith. Does God exist? The question, 'How many teachers at Parklands Comprehensive School believe that God exists?' is an empirical question. There are some questions, many of them important, which cannot be answered by empirical research, that is, by reference to sensory data. Part of the discipline of doing research is to recognize this necessary limitation of science. Science cannot answer all our questions. It can only answer empirical questions. The discipline of doing research requires that empirical questions be asked. Questions which have sensory, countable, measurable answers. How many? How often? At what speed? How long?

The first discipline required by the research process is to ask the right kind of questions. Researchable questions are limited in scope and very specific. Researchable questions are also empirical questions. They have touchable, countable, measurable answers. It can be a real challenge to devise a clear, specific, narrow, empirical question. This skill can be learned. You can learn to take a general question and formulate from it a research question. You will get more practice in the next chapter.

Honesty and accuracy

The second major discipline required by research is to be honest and accurate. Honesty and accuracy should be characteristics of any intellectual enterprise. Yet it takes a degree of self-control. We often have an outcome in mind. For example, we might believe that more students should consider the Tower of London to be more beautiful than Edinburgh Castle. But this second discipline in doing research compels us to be as objective as possible, to make sure that there is no bias in the way we ask questions, to ensure that we correctly record the data and are honest in reporting the results.

What is wrong with the following?

1 Here are pictures of two buildings. You really don't think the one on the left (Edinburgh Castle) is more beautiful, do you?

Write an unbiased version of this question.

2 Only seventy per cent of those asked thought that Edinburgh Castle was more beautiful than the Tower of London.

Write an unbiased statement of this research finding.

If we are disciplined and report accurately the findings of our research, then we increase the reliability of the research process. Some research has fallen into disrepute because researchers have not been disciplined, accurate, and honest. Have you ever read a report of controversy over scientific work in which bias has been suggested? An example would be Eysenck's research into racial differences in intelligence. What about the criticisms of Piaget's work? Some people have forced their data to fit their theory by falsifying results or not recording data accurately or both. Research is useful only to the extent that the researchers have been disciplined, accurate, and honest.

Record keeping

A third discipline required of a researcher is to record what was done in such a way that someone else can see exactly what was done and why. There are two reasons for this. First, it is one of the safeguards of the reliability of the research process. If what was done is reported in this way, some other person can repeat the research. If they get the same results, then what was found originally becomes even more certain. If they dó not get the same results, then the original findings are less certain.

The second reason for recording accurately and in detail what was done, what decisions were made and why, is to provide a record for yourself. It is amazing how quickly we forget what we did and why. At the end of the research you need to be able to refer to your research notes and refresh your memory; it is a great help when you are writing the limitations of the study.

Accepting limitations

The fourth and final discipline of the research process involves accepting the limitations of the research done. We will develop this idea later. If you study only one family, you cannot apply your findings to all families. If you study a group of 10-year-old boys your findings apply to that group and that group only. It is a great temptation to over-generalize, to make claims beyond the data actually collected.

Similarly, if you began your research with a non-empircal question, one of morality, or aesthetics, or religion, but did your research on an empirical question derived from the non-empirical question, your conclusions apply only to the empirical question. For example, if your initial question was, 'Is the Tower of London more beautiful than Edinburgh Castle?' but your research question was, 'How many Manchester secondary school students consider the Tower of London to be more beautiful?' the data you collect will answer the empirical question, not the question of beauty. Keeping your conclusions at the level of the questions asked is part of the discipline of accepting the limitations of the research process.

In summary, doing research requires that several disciplines be learned. The right kind of questions must be asked. Narrowly defined, focused questions are essential. In addition, only empirical questions can be answered by empirical research. Secondly, honesty and accuracy in asking questions and reporting findings is required. Thirdly, careful record-keeping and accurate reporting is needed. Finally, the researcher has to learn to accept the limitations of the research process.

Theory and data

Research is a disciplined process for answering questions about some aspect of the observable, touchable world. The question

can come from anywhere. We may just be curious. I wonder
how that works? I wonder why some people do this or that?
Does it make any difference? Curiosity can begin the research
process.

On the other hand a problem may motivate us to ask a
researchable question. How is the problem of teenage
malnutrition best handled? How can I make my father
understand me? How can I improve my health? How can the
incidence of drunken driving be reduced? Problems such as
these and many, many others motivate people to ask
researchable questions. Problems can get one started on the
research process.

Arguments are a frequent starting point. The example of
Mary and Frank is typical. We may have one idea about how
things are and you may have another. It may be possible to
design a piece of research to see whose idea is supported by
evidence. Research is often started by controversy. Columbus
set sail to the west in order to reach the East Indies and to test
the idea that the earth was not flat but in fact a ball. He risked
his life and those of his crew to test a theory, to settle a hot
controversy of his day.

Did Columbus discover evidence which proved the earth was
not flat? No. He did not reach the 'Indies'. He did not reach
the same place by sailing west as others had reached by sailing
east. Spain made itself rich on the gold from its conquests in
newly discovered lands. Magellan sailed around the world. He is
claimed to be the first European to do so. Was this evidence
uniformly accepted as proof that the earth was not flat and that
sailors who ventured too far would not fall off the edge? No.
Many people continued to believe that the earth was flat.
Perhaps satellite photographs of the earth taken from great
distances provide the most compelling evidence available to date
that the earth is not flat.

As with Columbus and the flat-earth theory, evidence does
not always stop the controversy that motivated research. Some
do not accept the evidence. Some argue that the research was
not properly conducted. Some argue that the research question
was not properly defined. In such cases the research process
usually goes on, with more and more evidence being collected to
test more carefully defined questions. Part of the fun of doing
research is to see how each question leads to more and more
questions. The research process is continuous.

The research process is a disciplined process for answering
questions. Another way of saying this is to say that the research

process is a disciplined process for relating theory and data. At this point we will try to clarify and simplify the terms 'theory' and 'data'.

Theory

Put most simply, a theory is a guess about the way things are. Mary had a theory about the fastest route to Leeds from Preston. A theory is an idea about how something works. A theory is an idea about what difference will be made by doing or not doing something. Theories are ideas about how things relate to each other. Theories are ideas.

There are many ways of expressing theories; some are very formal, others are informal. Some theories are very elaborate, complex, sophisticated, and mind-boggling. Yet simplicity and clarity are often desirable features of theories. Put most simply, theories are ideas about the way other ideas are related. Theories are abstract notions about the way concepts relate to each other. This will become clearer as you proceed through this book.

- A hunch about the fastest route between Preston and Leeds is a theory.
- An idea that putting a cup of salt into a litre of pea soup will make it too salty for your family is a theory.
- A guess that the more reassurance you give to small children that they are valued, cared for, and wanted, the more likely they are to develop healthy images of themselves is a theory.
- The saying, 'Spare the rod and spoil the child' is a theory.
- The idea that more education produces more reliable, more productive, more contented people is a theory.

A theory asserts a relationship between concepts. A theory states that things are related in a particular way. A theory is a statement of how things are thought to be. A theory is an idea, a mental picture of how the world might be.

The research process is a disciplined process for answering questions. The research process is a way of testing theories. The research process is a way of determining whether there is any evidence to support our mental picture of the way things are. The evidence collected by the research process is called data.

Data

Data are facts produced by research. Data, like facts, by themselves are meaningless. They take on meaning as they are related to theories. For example, the fact that Car A arrived in Leeds 30 minutes and 20 seconds before Car B is meaningless.

---

datum (singular) *data*, plural. Latin, neuter, past participle of *dare* to give. A thing given or granted, something known or assumed as fact, and made the basis for reasoning or calculation.

Shorter Oxford English Dictionary

The fact takes on meaning only when it is related to the two theories about which route is the faster from Preston to Leeds. The fact becomes part of the data by which these theories can be tested.

Data are facts. They are readings on thermometers. They are records of events (Car A arrived before Car B). They are counts (100 students thought the picture of Edinburgh Castle was more beautiful than that of the Tower of London). They are records of the actual state of some measurable aspect of the universe at a particular point in time. Data are not abstract, they are concrete, they are measurements of the tangible, countable, sensate features of the world. While theories are abstract mental images of the way things may be, data are measures of specific things as they were at a particular time.

The challenge of the research process is to relate theory and research in such a way that questions are answered. Both theory and data are required. When we are faced with a question we formulate a theory about its answer and test it by collecting data, that is, evidence, to see if our theoretical answer works. Data cannot be collected without some idea (theory) about the answer to the question. Theories alone are unsatisfactory because they are unproven, untested. To answer our questions we need both theory and data.

The end result of the research process is neither theory nor data but knowledge. Research provides answers to empirical questions as a result of evidence having been collected and evaluated. This is how we know. We ask questions, propose answers to them, and test those answers. Doing research in a disciplined way is how we know we know. The research process is a disciplined way of learning about ourselves and our world.

Questions for review

1 Why do we do research?
2 It is claimed that research is a process. What is a process?

3 What is the normal sequence of the research process? In what way is it normal?

4 What are the essential first steps of the research process? Why are the first steps so important?

5 What is done in Phase 2 of the research process?

6 What is done in Phase 3?

7 List the four major disciplines involved in the research process.

8 What are the two major properties of a researchable question?

9 What are theory and data? What role does each play in the research process?

10 Find a newspaper article or an article in a recent magazine which reports a controversy over research findings. What was the nature of the criticism of the research?

Phase 1
Essential first steps

Selecting a problem

The first phase of the research process involves selecting a
research problem, narrowing the focus of the question, selecting
a research design, defining and measuring variables, constructing
an investigating instrument, and drawing a sample. This phase is
one of decision-making, sorting, narrowing, and clarifying. It
requires clear thinking. This means that favourite ideas and pet
topics must be discarded for more precisely developed ideas.
This chapter deals with the discipline of selecting and refining a
topic for research.

Starting-points

The research process begins when our curiosity is aroused.
When we want to know something, we begin formally or
informally to engage in research. An observation, something
we read, a claim someone made, a hunch about something,
each may serve as a stimulus to begin the research process.
You may be assigned a topic or you may encounter an
examination question which asks you to design a piece of
research. In this chapter we will develop several examples
to demonstrate and to help you develop the skills required
to move from a starting-point to a focused researchable
question.

Here are some examples of the sort of things which might
serve as starting-points for research.

An observation
Some students get better marks than others.

An observation like this may prompt someone to ask such questions as: Why? Which students? Is it the way papers are marked? An observation may trigger the inquiring mind to ask questions and the research process has begun.

A family crisis
The Wright family has to decide whether to send their daughter to a state school or to a private school.

Someone who knows of this situation might be prompted to ask such questions as: What difference would it make? Is there a difference in terms of results? What kinds of factors do the Wrights consider important as they arrive at their decision? A situation, like a family crisis, may stimulate the asking of questions and the research process is under way.

A news report
Read the following article from the *Guardian*.

Couples' rights 'are best protected by marriage'
By Malcolm Dean

People who lived together could ensure that their property, financial, and social security rights were protected by getting married, Dame Margaret Booth, a High Court judge, said yesterday.

Dame Margaret, who has chaired a committee studying divorce procedure, told a seminar of judges and lawyers in London, organized by the American Bar Association, that there were difficulties in extending statutory protection to couples who cohabit.

'Surely it is up to them to consider whether they want a contractual agreement,' she said. Why should Parliament impose the rights and obligations of marriage on to couples who choose not to marry and take on the duties of spouses? The country was already subject to an ever-increasing number of laws, bylaws, and regulations.

Dame Margaret was responding to a paper prepared by Mr Robert Johnson, QC, chairman of the Family Law Bar Association, which calls for 'innovative legislation' to correct the injustices suffered by people who cohabited.

It argued that existing legislation was illogical and
arbitrary. The position of putative fathers was tenuous
and insecure, that of illegitimate children unequal and
unfair. Women cohabitees who had contributed regularly
to household expenses could be denied all property
rights.

Dame Margaret asked how the legislation would cope
with people who entered into two or three simultaneous
relationships. Did they want illegitimate children to have
precisely the same property and financial rights as
legitimate children?

If that was what was wanted why did people not face
the question of abolishing marriage?

A further difficulty was whether the law should be
restricted to heterosexual relationships.

Dame Margaret said no doubt there were deserving
couples who would be better served by a single legis-
lative code. There were some sad cases where a woman
emerged from a long relationship without security,
financial reward, or a roof over her head. But hard cases
made bad law.

American lawyers who spoke said there were 12 states in
the US which were ready to enforce contracts drawn up by
cohabiting couples. Other lawyers, in response to Dame
Margaret's comments said some cohabiting couples could
not marry. A spouse who was being denied a divorce in
Britain had to wait five years before divorce and
remarriage.

Mr Henry Hodge, a London solicitor, said it would not
be as difficult as Dame Margaret suggested to draft
legislation to protect cohabitees. The administrative law
had developed a detailed definition of cohabitation to deal
with social security claimants.

The Guardian, 19 July 1985

Do any questions come to your mind? There are a lot of
points in the article, but relatively little evidence. You might be
motivated to ask some questions about unmarried couples living
together. How common are such relationships? How successful
are they? Do the people involved tend to get married later on?
Precisely what are the advantages and disadvantages and how
do these compare with the situation in the past? The research
process is begun when enquiring minds ask questions. Anything,
including newspaper reports, can begin this process.

A policy issue
The government is concerned about the provision of proper
care in homes for elderly people.

Think about this issue. What questions does it raise? What is
the current state of affairs in homes for elderly people? What
do elderly people need? Again the enquiring mind is prompted
to ask questions which might lead to research.

These are some ways in which you might be prompted to
begin the research process. It makes little difference where you
begin. The first step is to narrow the focus and clarify the issues
involved in the problem. None of the above starting-points is
sufficiently refined to provide a useful question as a guide to
research. The first step in the research process is to move from
the starting-point to a researchable question.

Narrowing and clarifying the problem

The goal of this step in the research process is a clear statement
of the issue to be studied. One form of such a statement is the
hypothesis, which we will examine later in this chapter. Other
forms include the research question or objective. The virtue that
hypotheses, research questions, and objectives all share is that
they are precise, narrowly focused statements. How do you get
there? There are no rules or simple recipes for deriving a
hypothesis from whatever it is you started with. This skill is
best learned by practice.

The first thing to do if we are to narrow and clarify a
problem question is to 'unpack' it. Most of the starting-points
above contain many issues and suggest many different avenues
of research. The questions we begin with are usually quite
complex. They may sound simple, but they are probably far
from it. If we are to narrow and focus the issues for research,
we have to list the issues involved in the question. We are then
in a position to choose from that list a question that will focus
our attention on a narrowed problem.

In the last chapter we provided some examples to demonstrate
the process of limiting or narrowing questions. We saw that
asking some questions about the original question can help.
Questions like the following may help to 'unpack' the question.

- What are the major concepts?
- What is happening here?
- What are the issues?

- Is one thing affecting, causing, or producing a change in something else?
- Why is this so?

Such questions may help us to see what is going on and provide the information required to isolate the issues of particular interest. Take the example of the observation, 'Some students get better marks than others.'

One question to begin with is, 'Why does this observation hold?' Here are four possible explanations:

1 Some students are brighter than others.
2 Some students work harder than others.
3 Some students eat better meals than others.
4 Some students do better in English, while others are better at maths.

Using your general knowledge of students and marks, propose four more possible explanations for the observation that some students get better marks than others. Write them down.

Did you think of such possible factors as amount of time spent studying, adequacy of nutrition, native intelligence? Did you consider that there might be differences between subjects? If so, you have begun to 'unpack' the issue. You have begun to isolate factors and possible explanations. You have listed eight possible factors. It is unlikely that any research project of the size you will be asked to design or to do will address itself to any more than one or two of the factors. You can begin the narrowing by selecting just one factor. That will prove complicated enough.

Try your list again. What factors did you isolate as possibly relevant to differences in marks? Did you consider:

1 intelligence?
2 amount or quality of work?
3 nutrition?
4 the subject taken may make a difference?
5 others?
6
7
8

Each one of these factors could serve as the basis for a research project. It would be impossible to include them all. You have to narrow the focus of the research. After unpacking a question, you select from among the issues identified the one or two you plan to deal with.

A second suggestion to help you to narrow and clarify a question is to consult what has already been written about the topic. This is called reviewing the literature. You are almost certainly not the first person to have explored this area. What have others found? You may discover factors you had not thought of or learn of ways of approaching the problem you had not considered. You may also be relieved that others encountered difficulties similar to those you are having.

While you are clarifying and narrowing the research question you should at some point consult the literature available on the subject. The extent to which you do this will depend on the amount of time you have available. A full-scale search of the literature can be very time-consuming, and many of the books and articles you require will need to be obtained from other libraries. This can take several weeks, so you should allow plenty of time.

The starting-point of a literature search is the library catalogue. Most libraries have two catalogues, one which classifies books under authors and a classified catalogue which lists all books and pamphlets in the library according to topic. Some libraries list book titles with authors in a name or dictionary catalogue. Most libraries in the UK use the Dewey Decimal Classification Scheme. This divides up all knowledge into ten groups and gives each a number. The social sciences are classified from 300 to 399 as shown in Figure 3.1. These are then subdivided into more specific topics. Once you have discovered the Dewey Decimal numbers of the topic in which you are interested, by checking a subject index you easily find which books in this area the library possesses. At the same time you can check encyclopaedias such as the *International Encyclopaedia of the Social Sciences* and the *Encyclopaedia of Sociology*. These give brief surveys of particular areas and make suggestions for further reading, though these are inevitably somewhat dated.

For a fuller search you need to locate other books and articles. One way is to skim through past issues of journals which deal with your topic area; these may also be classified by their Dewey number. However, for a full search you need to make use of abstracts and indexes. These collect together details of articles from a number of journals and classify them under appropriate topic headings. In using abstracts you need to jot down key words before you start, because the article you want may have been classified under a different heading from the one you expect. For example, an article on costs in education may be classified under educational spending, or expenditure, or finance rather than costs.

Dewey Decimal Classification (19th edition)

300 The social sciences

301 Sociology
302 Social interaction
303 Social processes
304 Human ecology and
    demography
305 Social structure
306 Culture & institutions
307 Communities
308 —
309 (Social situation & conditions)
310 Statistics
311 —

312 Statistics of population

313 —
314 General statistics of Europe
315 General statistics of Asia
316 General statistics of Africa
317 General statistics of
    North America
318 General statistics of South
    America
319 General statistics of other areas

320 Political science

321 Forms of states
322 Relation of state to social
    groups
323 Relation of state to its residents
324 Electoral process
325 International migration
326 Slavery & emancipation
327 International relations
328 Legislation
329 Practical politics

330 Economics

331 Labour economics
332 Financial economics
333 Land economics
334 Cooperatives
335 Socialism and related systems
336 Public finance
337 International economics
338 Production
339 Macroeconomics

340 Law

341 International law
342 Constitutional & admin law
343 Miscellaneous public law
344 Social law
345 Criminal law
346 Private law
347 Civil procedure
348 Statutes, regulations, cases
349 Law of individual states and
    nations

350 Public administration

351 Central governments
352 Local units of government
353 United States federal & states
354 Other central governments
355 Military art & science
356 Foot forces and warfare
357 Mounted forces and warfare
358 Armored, technical, air, space
    forces
359 Sea (Naval) forces and warfare

360 Social pathology & services

361 Social problems & social
    welfare
362 Social welfare problems
363 Other social services
364 Criminology
365 Penal institutions
366 Association
367 General clubs
368 Insurance
369 Miscellaneous kinds of
    associations

370 Education

371 The school
372 Elementary education
373 Secondary education
374 Adult education
375 Curriculum
376 Education of women
377 Schools & religion
378 Higher education
379 Education and the state

380 Commerce	390 Customs and folklore
381 Internal commerce	391 Costume & personal
382 International commerce	appearance
383 Postal communication	392 Customs of life cycle,
384 Other systems of	domestic customs
communication and tele-	393 Death customs
communication	394 General customs
385 Railways	395 Etiquette
386 Inland waterway transportation	396 —
387 Water, air, space transportation	397 —
388 Ground transportation	398 Folklore
389 Metrology & standardisation	399 Customs of war & diplomacy

There are different editions of The Dewey Decimal Classification in use. Most libraries now use the 19th edition (1979) or the 18th (1971). Changes in the editions may mean different numbers for the same subject. For example, the sociology of women in the 18th edition is 301.412; in the 19th it is 305.4.

Figure 3.1 Outline of the Social Sciences Section of the Dewey Decimal Classification

A very useful British index is the *British Humanities Index*, which indexes articles from selected newspapers as well as from journals. Depending on your topic, other indexes may be more appropriate. You may find useful references in the *Social Services Abstracts*, produced by the DHSS, or in the *Abstract of Criminology and Penology*, *Housing Digest*, *International Political Sciences Abstract*, *Psychological Abstracts*, or *Sociological Abstracts*, to name just a few which may be relevant. The *British Education Index* and its American equivalent called *Education Index* are invaluable for those researching in this area. American works such as the *Review of Economic Literature* also cover British articles. If you are interested in newspaper articles the *Times Index* is a monthly index of articles in *The Times*, the *Sunday Times*, and the various *Times* supplements. Since 1981 the *Financial Times* has published a useful monthly index of its articles.

Only large academic and some public libraries will have all these indexes, but it is worth a special journey if you are undertaking research on a substantial scale. Such a library may also possess the *Social Sciences Citation Index*. This is a computer-based index to a wide range of social science journals. It concentrates on listing the references cited by authors and it can provide a very valuable source of information. However, it can be complicated to use and you may need the help of a librarian to get the best use out of it.

An increasing number of libraries offer computer on-line searches of large data bases such as BLAISE, URBALINE, ERIC, and SOCIAL SCISEARCH. An on-line search can save a great deal of time and effort, and it is worth inquiring if such a service is offered by the library.

Bibliographies are an essential tool if you wish to search out books on a particular topic. The *London Bibliography of Social Sciences* is based on the catalogue of the London School of Economics. UNESCO produce an *International Bibliography of the Social Sciences* with separate volumes for separate subjects such as economics, sociology, and political science. These may be held only in larger libraries, but the *British National Bibliography* and *Books in Print* are more widely available.

Other people may have researched your topic. *Dissertation Abstracts International* and the *ASLIB Index to Theses* list Ph.D. and Master theses, and research in progress is reported in *Research Supported by the ESRC*.

Undertaking a literature search is a difficult task, but it is a skill that can be learned. If you are just starting out you should begin by consulting an expert — a librarian. A good librarian is the finest resource available to anyone undertaking social science research.

You need not undertake a full library search at this early stage; as you clarify the problem you can narrow the search and at the same time extend it to less easily available sources.

Since narrowing and clarifying the problem is so important, let us take another example. Remember, the goal is a clear question for research. To do this you unpack your starting-point. List everything that comes to mind about the subject. Do some reading. Consult some people who are knowledgeable in the area. The more ideas the better. Then select one factor, one idea, one small problem for your research.

Let us try the example of a family crisis. The Wright family has to decide whether to send their daughter to a state school or to a private school.

This situation is quite complex. Remember that the aim is to isolate question for research, not necessarily to find an answer to the problem faced by the Wright family. What are some of the key concepts (ideas)? What issues are suggested? There are no right or wrong answers here. You are working toward a research question.

Here is a list of some of the issues, concepts, and factors this starting-point suggests to us.

1 Is one system of education demonstrably better than another
  in terms of sport?
  in terms of results?
  in terms of social life?
2 How do families make decisions like this?
  What factors do they consider?
  Do the children participate?
3 Do families consider boys and girls equally worth the expense
  of education?

What issues, further questions, factors occurred to you?
Write them down.

What resources do you have which might help you with this
question? Undertake a preliminary library search focusing on
topics such as costs in education, accountability, private
education (public schools), and also decision-making. Do some
preliminary reading to help you to focus on particular issues.
Then do a further library search and consult a librarian.

Again, once you have isolated some issues you can select one
and pursue it. The key at this point in the research process is to
identify issues, to select from all that is involved in a specific
issue or question that which you will pursue in depth, and to
leave the rest behind. We have seen that there are many issues,
ideas, and factors that might be raised by the decision to send a
daughter to a state or a private school. Your research will probably be able to treat only one. The rest must be left for another
study. It is the mark of a clear thinker and a good researcher to
be able to identify and note the *many* issues and to make the
choice to study *one*. People reading your report will realize that
you are aware of the complexity of the issues involved but are
sufficiently disciplined to address yourself to only one.

You may wish to gain more experience in narrowing and
focusing research questions by taking another of the starting-
points suggested earlier in this chapter. The basic approach is to
identify and write down all the issues, ideas, factors that come to
your mind when you think of the question, or situation, or news
report, or whatever it is that you started with. Background reading
will help you to think of issues, factors, and further questions.

Once you have listed the ideas and the factors that occur to
you, choose the ones you want to deal with. You might want to
examine the effect of different amounts of study time on
academic performance. You might want to examine the impact
of some aspect of nutrition on academic performance. You may
wish to explore some aspect of family decision-making. After

looking over the field, identifying the concepts and possible relationships among them, you select a few to work with.

Stating the problem

After you have isolated factors and issues, and have done some background reading about them, you will be ready to restate the issue as a researchable question. This is a skill in itself. We will discuss two basic forms, the hypothesis and the research objective. Most other forms can be seen as variations of either a hypothesis or a research objective.

The hypothesis

A hypothesis is a statement which asserts a relationship between concepts. A concept is an idea that stands for something, or represents a class of things. While some people define things differently, the definitions we have chosen are widely accepted, clear, and relatively understandable. The key feature of a hypothesis is that it asserts that two concepts (ideas) are related in a specific way. Usually a hypothesis takes the form 'X causes Y', or 'X is related to Y'.

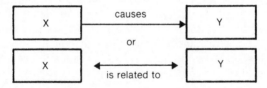

The usual form of a hypothesis

Let us return to the example we have been using. We began with the observation, 'Some students get better marks than others.' We have unpacked this observation by listing things that come to our minds. We thought of the possible impact of factors like amount of study, nutrition, or which subject was examined. We talked with teachers and read some material given to us by the librarian. When that was all done, let us suppose that we decided to do some research in the area of the impact of amount of study on marks. We have two concepts, study and marks. We also have an idea about how these two concepts are related. We suspect that the more one studies, the better marks one will receive.

Given all that preparatory work, we are in a position to write a hypothesis to guide our research, for example,

The more a student studies, the better will be the student's academic performance.

This hypothesis states that two *concepts*, namely amount of study and academic performance, are related in such a way that more of one (study or X) will produce or lead to more of the other (academic performance or Y). This hypothesis could be represented, or 'diagrammed', as follows:

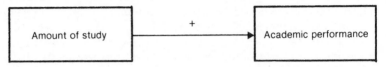

The two concepts are in boxes. The boxes are linked by an arrow going from one concept to the other. The arrow indicates that one concept (amount of study) does something to the other concept (academic performance). The plus sign indicates that the relationship is seen as a positive one, that is, that more of the one will lead to more of the other.

Diagramming hypotheses is a very useful device to promote clear thinking. If you cannot diagram your hypothesis, it may be because it is not yet clear to you. If you can, you are beginning to understand the issue.

Let us take a different example. We have diagrammed a positive relationship between two concepts. How about a negative one? Look over your list of factors that might affect academic performance. Is there one of which it could be argued that more of it would lead to lower academic performance? How about parties attended? The hypothesis would be stated:

The more parties a student attends, the lower will be the student's academic performance.

It would be diagrammed:

A hypothesis states that there is a relationship between two concepts and specifies the direction of that relationship. The above hypothesis states that there is a negative relation between attending parties and academic performance.

Let us continue with the 'factors affecting marks' example. Suppose that in doing your literature review on the factors affecting marks you came across an article that claimed that the kind of breakfast students ate had an effect on their academic performance. Write a hypothesis derived from this article.

Now diagram this hypothesis in the form below.

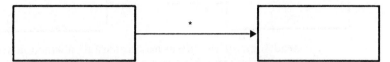

*Is the relationship proposed by the hypothesis positive or negative? If it is positive, place a plus sign in the blank. If it is negative place a minus sign in the blank.

The best way to develop skill in deriving hypotheses is to practise. Do the following exercises and then do this type of exercise using other topics and issues.

1 Here is a hypothesis: 'As the idea of unmarried couples living together becomes more widely accepted, there will be an increase in the number of couples cohabiting.' What are the key concepts?

- acceptance and
- number of couples cohabiting

What relationship between these concepts does this hypothesis assert?

Diagram this hypothesis here:

*Is the relationship proposed by the hypothesis positive or negative? if it is positive, place a plus sign in the blank. If it is negative place a minus sign in the blank.

2 Suppose you decided to pursue a comparison of satisfaction obtained by couples cohabiting compared to those who are legally married. You might propose the following hypothesis:

Being legally married increases the probability that couples will report high levels of satisfaction in their relationship.

Diagram this hypothesis here:

3 If you read some of the literature on marital satisfaction you would have discovered that there are many factors influencing marital satisfaction. Some of these factors are:

- values shared
- common backgrounds
- economic security
- security in the relationship
- emotional health of partners
- number of friends
- length of the relationship

One hypothesis which could be derived from these factors would be:

Couples who are legally married have more security in the relationship than couples who cohabit.

Diagram this hypothesis:

4 Derive another hypothesis from the above list of factors and write it out concisely.
Diagram it here:

As you can tell from doing these exercises, developing a hypothesis requires that you identify one concept or thing that causes, affects, or has an influence on another thing or concept. This is basic to the logic of a hypothesis. The concept that does the causing is called the *independent concept*. An independent concept is the thing that causes, produces a change in, or acts upon something else. The something else which is acted upon, produced, or caused by the independent concept is called the *dependent concept*.

Writing a hypothesis requires that you identify an independent concept and a dependent concept. An independent concept is the thing that causes, or acts upon, something else. In the earlier examples, amount of study, parties attended, and nutrition were independent concepts. These concepts were seen as causally related to, that is capable of producing a change in, academic performance.

List the independent concepts in the exercise you have just done on pp. 39–42. For example,

Exercise 1 acceptance
Exercise 2 marital status/being legally married
Exercise 3
Exercise 4

In terms of the diagram, the independent concept is the one *from which* the arrow is drawn.

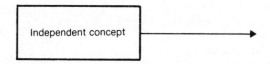

A dependent concept is the thing which is caused, is acted upon, is affected, in which a change is produced, by the independent concept. In the earlier examples, marks were the dependent concept. Academic performance was the thing affected by study or party going.

List the dependent concepts in the exercises you have just done on pp. 39–42. For example,

Exercise 1 marital happiness
Exercise 2 security in the relationship
Exercise 3
Exercise 4

In the pattern of diagramming introduced above, the dependent concept is the one *to which* the arrow is drawn.

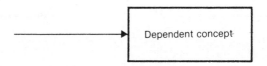

Hence

In its usual form a hypothesis states that something about the independent concept produces a change in the dependent concept.

Some of the confusion about independent and dependent concepts arises from the fact that it is possible for the same concept to be an independent concept in one hypothesis and a dependent one in another. Just because a concept is independent in one case does not mean that it should always be treated as independent. Try the following example.

Here are some concepts:

- academic performance
- nutritional adequacy of breakfast
- study
- party going
- intention to go to university

These concepts can be linked in a wide variety of ways. Many hypotheses can be derived from this list. We have seen that:

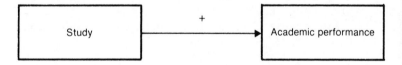

Which of the above concepts is the independent concept? Which is the dependent?

We have also seen that:

Which of the above concepts is the independent concept? Which is the dependent?

But it also makes sense to derive the following hypothesis using two concepts in the above list.

The greater the academic performance of a secondary school student, the more likely it is that the student will intend to go to university.

This hypothesis would be diagrammed as follows:

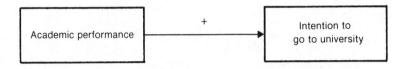

In this case, what had been a dependent concept (academic performance) in one hypothesis becomes an independent concept in this one, because going to university is dependent on academic performance whereas, earlier, academic performance was dependent on study. Whether a concept is independent or dependent depends on your theory, your idea of what is happening. Forming hypotheses and diagramming them helps to clarify theories.

Once you get the knack of forming hypotheses and diagramming them you can begin to explore new patterns involving more than two concepts. Using the concepts in the list above, the following are possible.

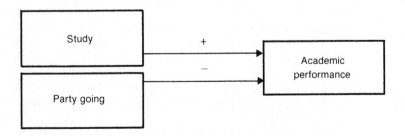

In this case two concepts, study and party going, are related as independent concepts to the dependent concept academic performance. One of the independent concepts is seen to be positively related and the other negatively related to the dependent concept.

Another possibility would be:

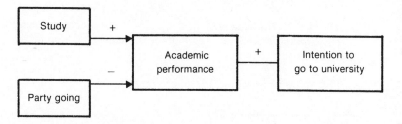

The concepts in this theory are related in such a way that study and party going affect academic performance, which in turn affects intentions to go to university.

The possibilities are endless. While the most complex theories can be diagrammed, most research projects deal with only one small aspect of the whole diagram. It is often a useful discipline to diagram more than you plan to study in order to show where the proposed research fits in the larger frame of reference. It will become clear as you work through this book that designing research to test the relationship between just two concepts is complex enough without adding more.

The research objective

Not all research is best guided by a hypothesis. Some research is done just to find out what is going on. In some cases it is not possible or desirable to try to specify the relationship among variables beforehand. There are times when developing a research objective may be a more desirable way to narrow the focus of a research project. For example, if the general area of your study relates to growth, development, or the acquisition of skills, you might use the following research objective to guide your research.

Objective: To observe a particular child, 4 years of age, for a specified period of time, in order to observe patterns of play.

When the goal of the research is descriptive rather than explanatory, a statement of research objective can serve to guide the activities of the research. Consider this example.

Objective: To describe what factors the Wright family took into account in making the decision to send their daughter to a state or a private school.

The intent of this research is simply to *describe* what happened, not to *explain* what happened. The researcher will at the end of the study be able to specify the factors which emerged in this family discussion. Who raised which issues? Who responded and in what ways? These observations might prompt the researcher to formulate a hypothesis which could be tested in another piece of research.

The starting-point on p. 32 which dealt with the policy issue of care for elderly persons might prompt research which is primarily descriptive. When you want to describe what is going on, an objective will help to focus your efforts. Here are some examples of research objectives related to care for the elderly.

Objective: To determine the number and percentage of elderly people in a particular community who require special accommodation.

The goal of this study is simply to find out the specific community need. There are no influencing factors under study. There is no attempt to test the impact of anything or whether special accommodation is needed.

Objective: To discover the existing policy on admission to homes for elderly people.

Objective: To discover the government's policy on funding for homes for elderly people.

So long as your aim is to describe what is, rather than to test explanations for what is, a research objective will provide an adequate guide to your research. We suspect that you will find that most research requires a hypothesis. It is difficult to stay at the descriptive level and not speculate or propose reasons, or begin to expect differences. A hypothesis becomes a better guide to research when you want more than a description.

Summary

The research process may be started from any point. Curiosity, claims of others, reading, problems, all can begin the process. Once begun, the first step is to clarify the issues and to narrow the focus of the concern.

In order to succeed, research must be guided by a clear statement of the problem or issue to be addressed by the research. The two most common forms such statements take are the hypothesis and the research objective. A research objective states the goal of a study which is intended to *describe*. A hypothesis is developed to guide research intended to test an *explanation*. Without a clear statement of the problem the research undertaken will be confused and ambiguous. It is impossible to proceed to the next stage of the research process in a satisfactory way without such a statement.

Questions for review

1 List six common starting-points for the research process.
2 What are the reasons for reviewing the literature on a particular subject?
3 Why is it essential to identify the issues or factors involved in a subject, topic, or problem being considered for a research project?
4 Why is it necessary to select one issue from among the issues identified?
5 What is a hypothesis? Give an example. Diagram a hypothesis.
6 What is a negative relationship? Give an example. How is it diagrammed?
7 What is a positive relationship? Give an example. How is it diagrammed?
8 What is an independent concept? What is a dependent concept? Which of the following are independent concepts? Which are dependent concepts?

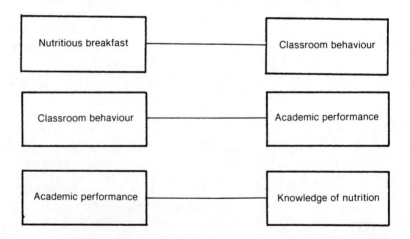

9 Write out fully each of the above diagrammed hypotheses.
10 Diagram the following:
  ● People of higher social class will have more books in their homes than people of lower social class.
  ● The introduction of a module on management theory will improve the quality of decision-making among students.
  ● The greater the age gap between parents and children the greater will be the degree of difficulty in communication they experience.
11 What is a research objective? How is it different from a hypothesis? For what kinds of research is it appropriate?

Selecting variables

Concepts and variables
Finding variables for concepts: hypotheses
Finding variables for concepts: research objectives
The question of validity
An overview of the research process
Questions for review

Once you have developed a hypothesis, you are ready to design some research to test that hypothesis. Similarly, once you have devised a research objective, you are ready to design a plan of research that will provide evidence to meet the objective. Up to this point we have stayed at the level of ideas, at the conceptual level. We have not asked how we are to measure the concepts in our hypothesis or objectives. That is, we have not yet determined how we are to collect empirical evidence.

As you recall from Chapter 2, the act of doing research involved asking empirical questions. Researchers ask questions which have sensory answers. The questions we ask as researchers must have answers that can be touched, counted, recorded, or in some way observed. Finding ways of measuring concepts demands creativity and skill. It is one of the more challenging aspects of doing research.

Concepts and variables

Up to this point we have dealt with concepts; academic performance, study, nutrition, marital happiness. These are abstract ideas. If we are going to do research involving these concepts we will have to find ways of making these abstract concepts concrete and measurable. The activity of finding measurable variables for concepts is called 'operationalization'. An operational definition of a concept goes beyond a usual dictionary definition. It defines a concept in terms that can be measured, that is, in empirical terms.

The basic question which guides this activity is: 'How can I measure that?' What can I take as an indicator of what is going on? Most of the concepts which concern us are not directly measurable. For example, when we want to know how hot something is we do not measure heat directly, we take its temperature. We agree that the changing height of a column of mercury in a tube will tell us what the temperature is. From the temperature we infer how hot a room is, a day is, a roast is, or a baby's fever is. The fact that temperature is an arbitrary scale of numbers having no direct relationship to how hot things are was made dramatically clear when they metricated our weather reports. We had to learn how hot 22° C felt.

In this case heat is the concept, the idea. How do we measure heat? We use thermometers. The thermometer is the measuring device. The scale of temperatures, be it Fahrenheit or Celsius, or something else, is the range along which measures are taken. Heat is the concept. Temperature is the variable, the thing that has more or less of something measurable. We operationalize the concept heat by the use of the variable temperature and measuring devices called thermometers. Temperature is an operational definition of the concept heat.

Let's pick up our sample hypothesis. When we last left it, it looked like this:

This hypothesis says two concepts, study and academic performance, are related in such a way that the more of one, study, the more there will be of the other, academic performance. The question we now face is, how shall we measure study and academic performance? What measurable, tangible, observable things can we take as indicators, things that point to study and academic performance?

Let's take academic performance first. We are so familiar with ways of measuring academic performance that we often forget the concept being measured. The measures with which we are most familiar include:

- marks
- test results

- essay marks
- teacher's reports
- project assessments

Academic performance is the abstract concept. Marks and test results are variables related to the concept of academic performance.

Variables

What is a variable? A variable is a concept that varies in amount or kind. A variable is a concept of which it is possible to have more or less, or different kinds. The variables that interest us are variables which not only vary in amount or kind but which are also measurable. For example, someone might say that love is a variable—you can have more or less of it and there are different kinds of love. However, love is not directly measurable. If we try to measure love we have to find suitable and measurable variables to use. Some might choose such measurable variables as the number of kisses received from one's lover or spouse, the frequency and quality of flowers received. The number of hugs, or the failure to remember important dates such as birthdays and anniversaries. While love itself is not directly measurable, we tend to find some measurable variables to assess whether we are loved or not.

The same is true of academic ability. Academic ability is measured by assessing the results of academic performance. A student's academic ability is assumed to be indicated by his or her performance on tests, essays, and projects. These are usually graded. Marks vary over a specified range (0–100, or ABCDEF, or Pass/Fail). Marks are taken as indicators of academic performance. Just as the readings from a thermometer are taken as indicators of how hot something is, marks or exam results are taken as indicators of the academic performance of a student.

What about study? How shall we measure study? What variables can be taken as indicators of study?

- Amount of time spent in revision.
- Amount of time spent practising.

It is hard to measure such things as concentration, or the absorption of material. But we can measure the amount of time a student spends 'studying'. Hence an operational definition of the concept study might be number of hours spent in revision.

It is now possible to state our hypothesis in two forms, in a conceptual form and in an operational form.

Conceptual form of the hypothesis

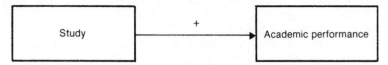

In its conceptual form the hypothesis asserts that there is a relationship between concepts, in this case, study and academic performance. In this form, study is the independent concept and academic performance is the dependent concept.

Operational form of the hypothesis

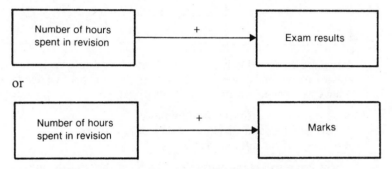

The operational form of the hypothesis asserts that there is a relationship between *variables*—in this case, number of hours spent in revision and exam results or grades. In this example, number of hours spent in revision is the independent variable and exam results, or marks, are dependent variables.

Any hypothesis can be stated at both the conceptual (or abstract or theoretical) level and at the operational (or empirical or measurable) level. At the theoretical level, a hypothesis asserts a relationship between concepts and at the empirical level it asserts a relationship between variables. We will practise deriving variables as appropriate measures of concepts, then we will discuss the problem of the relationship between concepts and variables.

Finding variables for concepts: hypotheses

There are no set ways or even useful guides for finding variables that are appropriate measures for concepts. This is an area for creativity and experimentation. Doing research involves a great deal of inventiveness and a willingness to think in new ways. You have to search for variables. Variables must be measurable and relate in some accepted way to the concept in question. Beyond those two rules, the job (or fun) of finding variables is up to you.

Here is another theoretical hypothesis, that is, a hypothesis stated at the conceptual level.

People with similar views are more likely to become friends than people whose views differ.

Diagrammed, the hypothesis looks like this:

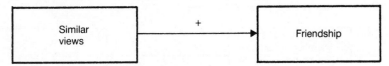

If we are to test this hypothesis we must find one variable that relates to people's views, and another that relates to friendship. Views can be shown in several ways:

● scores on an attitude questionnaire
● lists of likes and dislikes
● ratings of an interviewer

There are also several variables which can be used to measure friendship:

● number of meetings per week
● time spent together
● ask people to rate their friends on a scale

You may be able to think of others.

Taking one of the variables relating to views and one of those relating to friendship, restate the hypothesis relating views to friendship at the empirical or observable level.

The more similar their scores on an attitude questionnaire, the more time people will spend together.

Now in diagram form:

In this case what is the independent variable and what is the dependent variable?

For further practice, take two other variables, one related to views and one related to friendship. Develop an operational hypothesis and write it out.

Diagram it.

Now let us try an entirely new hypothesis. Take the area of family life. We are concerned about the relationship between resources and family well-being. We may have the theoretical hypothesis:

The more resources available to a family, the happier that family will be.

Diagram this theoretical hypothesis:

Think of variables that might be useful indicators, or specific measures of family resources. Things such as:

1 money
2 time
3 housing
4 relatives
5 social position

Now, what variables might be taken as indicators of family happiness? Happiness is one of those concepts which are not directly measurable. But we can get some indication. How? How about:

• absence of divorce?
• presence of observable signs of affection—hugs, kisses?
• self-reported happiness?
• the result on a test of marital happiness?

Think of other indicators of family happiness.

One operational hypothesis which can be derived from the above list of variables is:

The more time a family spends together the less likely it is to be split by divorce.

This could be diagrammed as follows:

Note that although the theoretical hypothesis asserts a positive relationship between two concepts, this operational hypothesis asserts a negative relationship between two variables. This is not a problem. Divorce is taken as a negative indicator of marital happiness. Here is another possible operational hypothesis.

The more time a family spends together the more likely are members of the family to report that they are happy with the family.

This hypothesis would be diagrammed:

Gain some practice by deriving other operational hypotheses from the above lists of variables and diagram them.

Finally, let us take one more example. Many people are interested in the differing behaviours of men and women. One area in which there seems to be a difference is in interest in politics. This example is a useful one to explore because it deals with a kind of concept and variable we have not seen to this point—the *categorical* concept or variable. A categorical concept or variable is one that is rigidly divided into two or more exclusive categories. Examples of categorical variables include:

- male v. female
- single v. married v. divorced
- middle class v. lower class
- state school v. private school

- employed v. unemployed
- atheist v. believer

Our theoretical hypothesis might be:

Men are more interested in politics than women are.

Unlike other kinds of variables, categorical variables are not stated as more or less, but as one or the other. You don't classify people as more or less female, but as either male or female. So the independent concept in the above hypothesis is a categorical hypothesis.

Usually categorical concepts are measured by categorical variables. While this is not necessarily so, it is usually so. Hence the independent variable in most operational hypotheses derived from the above theoretical hypothesis will involve a categorical independent variable, namely, male or female. The first half of a diagram of an operational hypothesis, the part showing the independent variable will look like this:

The problem now becomes one of how to select some variable which relates to 'interest in politics'. Several could be chosen, for example:

1 attends political meetings
2 votes
3 joins political party or pressure group (e.g. CND)
4 reads political pages of newspapers
5 scores high marks on a test of political knowledge

Thus one possible theoretical hypothesis would be:

Males are more likely to attend political meetings.

This would be diagrammed:

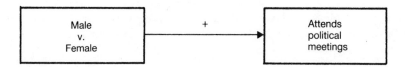

An operational hypothesis related to this theoretical hypothesis could be stated:

In the four weeks up to the next general election, males will be more likely than females to attend meetings arranged by election candidates.

Again this hypothesis would be diagrammed:

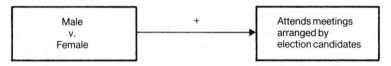

Note that this hypothesis is focused on a narrow area; for example, it does not deal with the causes of any differences.

To gain more practice in selecting variables we suggest that you identify other issues, formulate conceptual hypotheses, and then try to identify appropriate variables.

Finding variables for concepts: research objectives

We have considered research objectives. Let us have a further look at objectives at this point. When developing research to meet our objectives it is still necessary to clarify our concepts and to select variables appropriate to these concepts. For example, the research objective might be:

To learn about infant growth and development.

Growth and development are the concepts. The question that needs to be answered is what variables relate to growth and development. Growth is fairly easy. Weight, height, length of limbs, are all variables that relate to growth. By observing changes in these variables we can make inferences about growth.

What variables relate to development? We can now see that the above objective is still very broad. What kind of development — psychosocial, behavioural, sensorimotor? For each of these and other kinds of development there are well established variables to observe. Specific abilities, or patterns of behaviour, are taken as evidence of one or another kind of development.

Research objectives are used to guide research that seeks to *describe* as opposed to research that seeks to *explain* what is happening. While this means that there will not be independent and dependent concepts and variables, it is still necessary to operationalize the concepts in the research objective. Variables must be selected to serve as indicators for the concepts being studied.

Another objective presented in the last chapter was:

Objective: To discover the existing policy on admission to homes for elderly people.

At first glance this one seems perfectly straightforward. Go and find out. Find out what? Policy is a fairly general concept. How might admission policy vary from home to home?

- age
- health
- financial status
- family status

All of these are variables related to the concept policy. Put differently, they are aspects of admissions policies to homes for the elderly which might vary. By thinking through these issues before beginning *your* data collection, the research is focused and clarified. Some background reading, or reviewing the relevant literature, will help to identify variables that might be related to the concepts under study.

Another example of a research objective may help to demonstrate further the idea that both hypotheses and research objectives deal with concepts. In order to study concepts empirically, which is what research is all about, it is necessary to identify variables which are related to the concepts being studied.

Objective: To observe the classroom behaviour of top infants.

What aspect of classroom behaviour is to be observed? Classroom behaviour is the concept. What might be some variables related to the classroom behaviour of top infants? Some of the following variables might be considered:

1 attention span of each child
2 noise level in classroom
3 frequency of discipline
4 attention span of the whole class
5 frequency of disruptive behaviour
6 length of time taken to settle down at beginning of lesson

Before beginning an observational study it is necessary to decide what is to be observed. This involves selecting a few variables related to the concepts being studied.

The question of validity

We have discussed the challenge of finding variables to serve as measurable indicators for our concepts. We have moved from the abstract theoretical level to the empirical and measurable level. We must question all the variables we use to provide indicators of our theoretical concepts: How good is each possible indicator? Does it adequately reflect our concept? Or is it partial? Is it not quite the same thing? This is the issue of validity. Does the variable as measured adequately reflect what interests us in the concept?

Many arguments arise over the issue of validity. Take the case of IQ testing. Do the tests validly reflect innate intellectual ability? Or do they test something else? Take the issue of results. Do exam results validly reflect academic performance? Or do they measure something else? Is attendance at meetings really a valid measure of interest in politics? Can the absence of divorce be taken as an indication that a family is happy? Were you satisfied with the variables suggested as measures for love— number of kisses, hugs, flowers, or anniversaries remembered?

Wherever we feel dissatisfied with the variables chosen to measure a concept we raise the issue of validity.

- Is a low noise level a valid indicator that a class is learning? Or is it just well-disciplined?
- Is the fact that a baby gains a great deal of weight quickly a valid indicator of its health, or of the calorie content of its diet?
- Is an expressed opinion a valid indicator of the way a person will act?
- Is church-going a valid indicator of depth of spirituality? Or is it an indicator of conformity? Or of something else?

This is the problem of validity. When we move from the abstract to the concrete we encounter problems. It is not obvious. Not everyone will agree with our selection of variables. One of the things that need to be stated in the research report under the heading of limitations is any problem you feel about the degree to which your theoretical concept is adequately covered by the variable you selected. This is not a matter of finding the 'perfect' variable. There is none. It is a matter of finding an adequate variable and being honest about its possible shortcomings.

An overview of the research process

What have we learned so far? It is important that we keep the various threads of development together. From time to time we will try to give an overview of the research process.

When we encounter a problem, or a question about which we want to do some research, we first try to express that concern in a research objective or a hypothesis. This activity focuses our attention. It clarifies our interest. When stated as a hypothesis our focal question, or statement of concern, asserts a relationship between two or more concepts. When stated as a research objective, our focal question defines, using concepts, our area of interest. We examined such sample hypotheses as:

The more a student studies, the better will be his or her academic performance.

People with similar views are more likely to become friends than people whose views differ.

Families that have access to more resources are happier than families with access to fewer resources.

These hypotheses are all stated at the conceptual level. Each hypothesis states a relationship between ideas.

By now we can see that whether our research is guided and focused by a hypothesis or by a research objective, we select variables as observable indicators for the concepts we are studying. One of the more challenging and creative tasks in the research process is the discipline of finding measurable, observable, sensory variables that relate to the concepts that concern us. The following flow chart may help to clarify the steps in the research process we have learned so far.

Step 1
Select, narrow, and focus the problem to be studied.
State problem as either a hypothesis or a research objective.

Step 2
Select variables that relate to the concepts in the hypothesis or research objective.

Step 3

As we go along we will fill in the additional steps that have to be taken.

The following table lays out some of the examples we have developed.

Concept	Variables related to concept
Academic performance	Marks Exam results Essay evaluation Teachers' reports
Similar views	Scores on an attitude questionnaire Lists of likes and dislikes Ratings of an interviewer
Interest in politics	Attends political meetings Votes Joins political party
Growth	Height Weight Length of limbs
Classroom behaviour	Attention span Degree of disruption

For each concept we have identified several related variables. For each idea we have suggested two or more measurable, observable indicators.

If the variable selected relates appropriately to the concept under study it is said to be a valid variable. The problem of validity deals with the success of our efforts to find measurable indicators of our theoretical concepts. One of the limitations usually discussed is the validity of the variables selected. How valid is this particular variable as an indicator of that concept? For example, how valid are test results as indicators of that concept? For example, how valid are teachers' reports as an indicator of academic performance? How valid is voting behaviour as a measure of interest in politics?

Questions for review

1 What is a concept? Give three examples.
2 What is a hypothesis?
3 What is a variable?

4 Why are variables selected?

5 Here are some concepts. For each one think of at least two variables.

Concept	Related variables
Health	
Marital happiness	
Satisfactory housing	
Maturity	
Study	
Socio-emotional development	
Poverty	

6 What is the difference between a hypothesis and a research objective? Why must variables be selected for both?

7 To what does the question of validity refer?

8 What is an operational definition? State the following hypothesis in an operational form.

The better a student's nutritional status the better will be that student's classroom behaviour.

5

Finding a variable's measurements

If we are studying infant growth, the selection of variables is fairly straightforward—length, weight, length of limbs, circumference of chest. We readily accept that changes in length and weight (usually increases) are useful indicators of an infant's growth. We accept length and weight as variables relevant to the concept growth. Moreover, we have no problem in measuring these variables. We use a scale to measure weight and report the variation in grams and kilograms or in pounds and ounces. The same is true for length. We use a metre- or yardstick and report the variation in length in centimetres or in feet and inches.

The logic of measurement

The simplicity of the examples of length and weight is both reassuring and misleading. It is reassuring because it shows that the logic of measurement is familiar to us. We use it every day and are comfortable with it. The simplicity of the examples of length and weight is misleading because it obscures the difficulty with which agreed-upon measures are derived. Standard measures of length and weight have been developed over centuries, but there is still disagreement as to the units of measure. For example, metric measurements are used in athletics events, but road signs show miles. On the other hand, because length and weight are simple to measure and are

64

familiar they provide good examples of the logic of measurement.

Figure 5.1 uses the example of physical growth to show the relationship between concepts, variables, measuring instruments, and units of measurement. This relationship is basic to all empirical research. In doing research we try to measure systematically some aspect of the world around us. To measure a variable we need both a measuring instrument and units of measure in which to report variations in measures taken.

Concept	Variable	Measuring instrument	Units of measure
Physical growth	length	metre stick ruler tape measure	metres, centimetres, or feet inches
	weight	scale	kilograms, grams, or stones pounds, ounces

Figure 5.1 Measurement: the example of physical growth

Figure 5.1 shows clearly the order in which the problems facing a researcher are ideally handled. We have been trying to follow that order in the presentation of material in this book. First, clarify the problem by defining the concepts to be studied. Secondly, identify variables associated with each concept. Select one or two variables for each concept. Thirdly, devise or select a measuring instrument for each variable. Fourthly, select or devise units of measurement for each variable. The logical order of issues to be dealt with is presented in Figure 5.2.

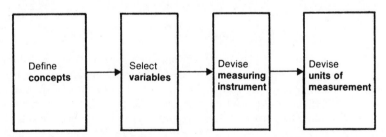

Figure 5.2 The logical order of issues to be decided in measurement

Some additional examples may help to clarify the logical flow of the issues related to measurement. As you look at the examples in Figure 5.3 try to think of other ways of measuring each variable, or of other units of measurement.

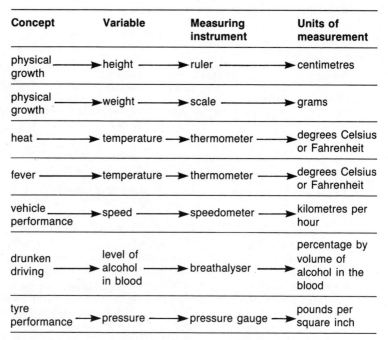

Concept	Variable	Measuring instrument	Units of measurement
physical growth ⟶	height ⟶	ruler ⟶	centimetres
physical growth ⟶	weight ⟶	scale ⟶	grams
heat ⟶	temperature ⟶	thermometer ⟶	degrees Celsius or Fahrenheit
fever ⟶	temperature ⟶	thermometer ⟶	degrees Celsius or Fahrenheit
vehicle performance ⟶	speed ⟶	speedometer ⟶	kilometres per hour
drunken driving ⟶	level of alcohol in blood ⟶	breathalyser ⟶	percentage by volume of alcohol in the blood
tyre performance ⟶	pressure ⟶	pressure gauge ⟶	pounds per square inch

Figure 5.3 Examples of the logical order of issues to be decided in measurement

The research process is a disciplined way to develop reliable knowledge about some aspect of the world around us. In the second chapter we noted that empirical research can deal only with those things that can be touched, or counted, or measured. We have learned that first we must clarify our ideas about the subject of our research. We do this by defining concepts clearly. Then we begin the movement towards measuring our concepts by selecting variables that relate to the concepts we wish to study. So far we have used examples from the physical sciences. What about measurements in the social and behavioural sciences?

Measurement in the social and behavioural sciences

As we learned in the last chapter, for each concept in our research objective or hypothesis we identify and select one or more variables. Once we have done this the issue becomes, how are we to measure the variation in the variables selected? The problem of measurement involves two issues:

1 By what instrument are we going to measure the variable?
2 In what units are we going to report the results of our measuring?

The discipline of the research process requires not only clear and focused thinking but careful and reliable measuring of the variables to be investigated.

It is unfortunate that in the social and behavioural sciences no truly standardized measures and scales have yet been developed. Yet there are some tools which are nearly universal. For instance, there are a number of measures of personality which are quite standard. Even with its acknowledged problems, IQ is a fairly standard scale. There are a number of tests of intelligence, but most report results according to a scale called the Intelligence Quotient or IQ. However, for the most part researchers in the social and behavioural sciences must develop their own measuring instruments and scales for reporting results.

This is part of the great challenge of doing research in the social and behavioural sciences. A great deal of creativity is demanded and permitted. Life as a researcher in this area would be simpler, although perhaps less interesting, if there existed generally accepted and standardized measures of:

- social class
- political attitudes
- marital happiness
- quality of life
- resources
- health
- nutritional status
- academic performance
- social adjustment
- learning
- effective management
- racial prejudice
- motivation

While some attempts have been made, usually they have been found to be lacking in one way or another. Measures of IQ seem to be affected by other factors such as class, or culture, or nationality. For example, a test measuring IQ which used questions related to urban life would not accurately indicate the IQ of a person from a rural area.

Whatever the area of research, be it physics or psychology, astronomy or botany, the researcher is essentially observing some aspect of the universe. Measuring our observations is important for two basic reasons. First, measurement enables us to systematize and record our observations. Secondly, measurement helps us to communicate our observations more clearly.

Compare 'My son is growing' with 'My son has grown 10 cm in 3 months.' Compare 'My daughter is doing better at school' with 'My daughter has received all As this year compared to a mixture of As and Bs last year.' Compare 'Today is warmer than yesterday' with 'Today's temperature at noon is 23° C compared with yesterday's temperature of 19° C.' Compare 'Rich people are more likely to send their children to private schools' with '78 per cent of parents with assets of over £x send their children to private schools.' Compare 'In my experience, people who eat a well-balanced diet are healthier than those who don't' with 'A study comparing two matched groups of 45-year-old male factory workers revealed that the group whose diet regularly included foods from all five food groups had lower blood pressure and a lower rate of dental caries than a matched group whose diet was mainly composed of fatty meat and simple carbohydrates.'

What do these comparisons indicate? In each case the first statement is an observation, a generalization drawn from experience. However, it does not use measurement. There are no reference points. There is no way of comparing that observation with other observations. The second of each pair of compared statements is precise and the measures used are clear. Without measurement we cannot make clear and comparable statements about the world around us. The use of measurement in making observations is one of two major factors that separate general impressions from the disciplined observations of the researcher. The other factor is making systematic and representative observations. We deal with this second factor under the topic of sampling. By using measurement we can become more consistent and reliable in both our observing and our reporting. Moreover, our observations can be reported to others. Research does not deal with vague impressions but with systematically measured and recorded observations.

There are three basic techniques used by researchers in the social and behavioural sciences to measure variables. The first technique is observation. Researchers observe what is going on and record what they observe. The second technique used to measure variables is interviewing. In the interview the researcher asks questions, someone responds, and the response is recorded. The third technique researchers use to gather data is to examine records and documents. Each of these techniques provides measurable, countable answers. We will examine each approach in turn.

Using observation to measure variables

One of the most basic techniques for gathering data is observation. To observe is simply to watch what happens. However, all observation, and particularly scientific observation, is guided by a question. Researchers do not just go and have a look; they are looking for something. What is looked for will depend in general on the hypothesis or the research objective. More importantly, what the researcher is looking for is best determined before the observation is begun. We will examine the requirement of a proper observational study.

First of all, decide what you will observe. This may seem obvious to some, but the following exercise will help to demonstrate the importance of deciding what to look for.

Take a look

This exercise is best done by a group. It can be fun for three or four or more people. Go with the group to some place: a pub, a classroom, a playground, a street, a football match, a party: almost any place will do.

Let everyone look at the scene selected for two minutes. This should be done quietly with no sharing of views. Then ask each person to write down everything observed. After each person has finished writing, share your observations. Then ask:

- What did you find?
- Was there much similarity in what was seen?
- Were there many differences in what was seen?

Normally when we look in a direction we do not see everything. We focus on those things that are relevant to us — cars if we are driving; trees if we are admiring the changing seasons; the sky if we are wondering about rain; the clock if we are unsure of the time. But we will look at a clock differently if we are deciding which clock to buy. What we see is guided by what we are looking for. In research it is important to be guided properly by well-focused questions.

An example may help to clarify this further. You are assigned the task of studying infant growth and development. As a good researcher you decided to focus on growth, thereby narrowing the field of your research and keeping the study within manageable bounds. Further, you decided to study one infant for a period of eight weeks. Your research objective was clearly stated as follows:

> To observe the physical growth of one infant over an eight-week period.

You had also decided to use length and weight as the measurable variables by which to indicate changes in physical growth. Hence, the operationalized restatement of your research objective would be:

> To observe changes in one infant's length and weight over an eight-week period.

A research objective stated as clearly as this one greatly facilitates research.

Now it is obvious in this case that you would not simply peer into the baby's cot once in a while to see if there had been any change in the baby's length or weight. Rather, you would ask, 'How long and how heavy is this baby?' at specified regular intervals during the eight weeks. It could be daily or weekly or fortnightly. You would have to record your data. A form such as the following would prove helpful. It is given as one example of a form which provides for systematic recording of measurements taken. Once completed, this form will provide a systematic record of observations. From it you can construct

Data recording form for observation of infant
growth

Infant's name: _____ Age: _____ Sex: _____

Week	Date	Infant Length	Weight
One			
Two			
Three			
Four			
Five			
Six			
Seven			
Eight			

graphs, charts, tables, or some other mode of presenting
your data.

If your study were, as the research objective indicated, a case
study of one infant, you would have one data record sheet like
the one above. If, however, you studied more than one infant,
you would have one form for each infant. It is essential to
record data separately for each infant in order to make
comparisons later.

From the above example you can see that to prepare for data
collection you need to:

1 Select concepts.
2 Select variables.
3 Select a means for measuring those variables.
4 Design a means for recording the measurements you will
make.

If all this is done before you begin to collect data, then data collection and analysis will proceed more smoothly and easily. Failure to measure and record your data will jeopardize the rest of the research process.

Think back over the example about infant growth. Ask yourself the following questions:

- What concept was being studied?
- What variables were selected?
- How was each variable measured?
- In what units of measurement is variation in each variable reported?
- What data recording devices were developed?

The research process has a logical flow. There is an order in which questions should be asked and answered.

Here is another example of a research project in which observation plays an important role. Assume that your hypothesis is:

Boys behave better in the classroom than girls.

What are the concepts involved in this hypothesis? The problem will be to find variables related to the concept of classroom behaviour.

This hypothesis requires that some measure of classroom behaviour be devised to ascertain whether boys behave better in class than girls. You have decided to conduct your research by observation rather than by interview or by the examination of records.

Note: It would be quite possible to conduct this research using either of the other techniques.

How are you going to measure classroom behaviour? There are many ways. It might be useful to observe a class for one period, just to see what kinds of things go on; to discover some possible variables. You might make a list of all the kinds of behaviours you observed. This is not to collect data to test the hypothesis, but to discover what variables can be observed and what kind of data can be collected. You will also discover some of the problems that are likely to arise. For example, will you be able to keep track of all the children in the classroom? Will you have to have several observers? Will you have to observe only a subgroup, a sample of the class? The following shows one approach to this problem:

Discovering what there is to observe

You are interested in measuring classroom behaviour. You must first obtain permission from a headteacher. While you are in the classroom write down all the behaviours you observe. For example:

- sitting still
- poking neighbour
- throwing something
- talking to neighbour
- interrupting
- reading
- writing
- dozing

When you have finished, ask yourself the following questions:

- Was I able to record all relevant behaviour?
- Was I able to keep the students straight in my mind? That is, could I remember which student had done what?
- Which of the behaviours I observed could be labelled desirable and which not desirable?
- How can I classify classroom behaviours?

Now that you are aware of some of the problems of observing classroom behaviour it is possible to devise a technique for measuring a variable that relates to the concept classroom behaviour. Ideally, every sort of behaviour of each student in the class would be recorded and coded as either desirable or undesirable. This is clearly very, very difficult.

A better approach would be to devise a list of disruptive behaviours. Each time such behaviour was observed in a class you could place a tick after the behaviour in one of two columns marked boy or girl. In this way data would be collected for the class as a whole, not for each student. Your observation checklist might look like this:

Observation checklist for classroom behaviour

Class: _____   Date: _____

Observer: _____   School: _____

Teacher: _____   Subject: _____

Behaviour	Boy	Girl
1 Pokes neighbour		
2 Talks out of turn		
3 Whispers		
4 Interrupts		
5 Gets out of desk		
6 Dozes		
7 Throws something		
8		
9		
10		
Total disruptive behaviour in this classroom		

This checklist focuses on disruptive behaviour in the classroom. Presumably, the variable becomes the amount of such behaviour exhibited. If girls exhibited more disruptive behaviour than boys, the hypothesis would be supported by the data collected. While this form was devised for observing one classroom, by using similar forms to observe behaviour in other classrooms, comparisons could be made.

In order to gain practice, devise an observation checklist for the observation of positive behaviour in the classroom.

While the above checklist compares boys and girls, it could just as well have compared other groups, for example older and younger children. Similarly, the setting could change to an assembly, or to a sports match, a café, or a concert.

The basic point is that an observation checklist helps to focus the observations and to facilitate systematic recording of observations. The behaviour or other events being observed become countable when collected this way. They become measurable variables. It becomes possible to move from an impression to facts. Instead of saying it was my impression that the girls were more disruptive in class than the boys, you would be able to say that girls were observed to engage in a number of disruptive acts while boys engaged in fewer disruptive acts. Another study could be done using the above observation checklist. It would compare boys and girls on type of disruptive behaviour rather than amount. The question would be 'Are boys disruptive in different ways from girls?' In this study:

- The basic concept would be classroom behaviour.
- The variable selected would be type of disruptive behaviour observed.
- The measuring device would be an observation checklist.
- The units in which variation in the variable would be reported would be types of disruptive acts displayed by boys compared with types of disruptive acts displayed by girls for a given period.

It is now possible to summarize some of the key points in collecting data, or finding a variable's measurements, by means of observation. First, if it is to be worth while, observation must be guided by a clear question and a clear identification of what is to be observed. One very handy way to do this is to devise an observation checklist. By using an observation checklist you can make that which is to be observed countable. You can report the number of times something happened or appeared. In this way you identify a variable related to the concept you are studying. You also quantify the variable under study. By the systematic recording of observations you develop a measuring instrument for the variables you are studying.

Secondly, it may be important to have more than one person do the observing. This is particularly true if there is a lot to observe. More detail may be recorded, ensuring greater accuracy.

Thirdly, it takes practice to develop the skills of observation. It cannot be done well by a person who is unfamiliar with the setting or the kind of action likely to be observed. If it is at all possible a few practice sessions are highly recommended before a session of observation for data collection is begun. It takes practice to weigh and measure a baby. It takes even more to learn to observe patterns of human interaction.

To recap, observation is the most basic data collection technique available to the researcher. The first difference between ordinary casual observation and scientific observation is that scientific observation is guided by a clearly stated question. The second difference is that researchers systematically record their observations in a way that makes the phenomenon under study countable. Instead of impressions, numerical data are recorded:

not: If shopkeepers cut their prices they would sell more,

but: A shop cut the price of cigarettes by 5 pence per packet. During the next week sales rose by 100 packets.

not: It is my impression that girls are better behaved in the classroom,

but: In one-hour observations conducted in each of 6 classrooms at _____ school, boys were found to exhibit an average of 16 disruptive acts per hour while girls exhibited 12 such acts.

Thus, one way of finding a variable's measurement is through systematic observation.

Some further examples of research using systematic observation to find a variable's measurement may help to develop your skills in observation. Suppose you were interested in the area of sex role differences in human interaction. Your background reading in this area has indicated that the opinions of women are frequently given less weight, ignored, or ridiculed by men. Moreover, you suspect that this 'putting down' occurs frequently in the context of the family. You decide to observe family interaction patterns in order to test the hypothesis that:

The evaluation of contributions to a conversation will be affected by the gender of the contributor.

This can be diagrammed:

Gender is, of course, a categorical variable. Someone is either male or female. The dependent variable poses a greater challenge.

But you, the researcher, have decided to focus on the evaluation of opinions expressed in a family context. You will explore the variable by asking the following questions:

- Is the opinion ignored?
- Is the opinion discussed further?
- Is the opinion ridiculed or scorned?
- Is the opinion discounted?
- Is the person interrupted?
- Is the person ignored?

How can you conduct the study? Let us assume that you have received the permission of a family to record its mealtime conversation. All you want is an audio recording of a normal meal in their home. The Sloan family consists of father, mother, and their two children, John who is 18 and Helen who is 16. Once you have the tape of the conversation you or you and several others can 'observe' what happened and fill out an observation checklist such as the one below for each person participating in the conversation:

An observation checklist for analysing a conversation

Person: _____

Type of conversation: _____

	Location on tape	Comment	Fate of comment							
			Rejected	Ridiculed	Ignored	Interrupted	Discussed	Praised	Adopted	
1										
2										
3										

The question is, 'What happens to each member's contribution to the conversation?' In the observation checklist note down where on the tape (using the counter on a tape recorder) the contribution began. Note the speaker. Then note what happened to the contribution.

By using a tape recording you can go back over the event and make sure you have it right. You can also have several people 'observe' the event and compare assessments. For example, let us assume that you recorded a mealtime conversation of the family described above. Part of the conversation might have gone:

Helen (trying to get a word in):   'I've got a problem.'
John: 'You always have problems' and continues speaking about Saturday's football match.

In this instance Helen's comment was ignored. The conversation continues:

Helen: 'Look, I've got to talk to you about . . . '
Father: 'Be quiet and let John finish.'

Here, Helen is interrupted and stopped by her father. If this pattern were to continue throughout the conversation, there would be some evidence to suggest that Helen was not taken seriously by male members of her family.

Once you have filled out a checklist for each person in the conversation you can compare the fate of the contribution of each member. You can compare parents with children, males with females. Mother with father and son with daughter. By comparing the number of negative fates (being ignored, discounted, ridiculed, or interrupted) with positive fates (discussed further, praised, adopted, taken seriously) it is possible to assess differences in the variable: evaluation of contributions to a conversation.

Thus, one way to measure a variable is by systematic observation. The following questions should be answered in order to ensure that the proposed observation will yield useful results.

A checklist for research involving observation

1 Have you clarified and narrowed your hypothesis or research objective? What are the key concepts?
2 What variables are to be studied?
3 How is each variable to be measured?
4 Have you devised an observation checklist, or some other means of systematically recording your observations?
5 Have you practised using your checklist?
6 In what units will the results be reported?

If you can answer these questions, you are probably ready to conduct your observations. You are not ready until you can.

Using interview schedules and questionnaires to measure variables

It is not always possible or even desirable to use observational techniques to collect data. Data are measures of variables. The second common data gathering technique used to measure variables involves asking people questions. In an interview, the researcher asks the respondent (the person being questioned) questions, in either a face-to-face situation or over the telephone, using an interview schedule. A questionnaire is used when the respondent reads and answers the questions separately from the interviewer. Both the interview schedule and the questionnaire are techniques for measuring variables which involve asking people questions.

We cannot overemphasize the fact that interview schedules and questionnaires are devices for measuring variables. Each question asked must have some intended bearing on one of the variables you are studying. These techniques are not fishing expeditions in which all sorts of 'interesting' questions are asked. There are two reasons for this. Pure curiosity is not an adequate motivation for putting a question on a questionnaire (or in an interview schedule). Secondly, what do you plan to do with the information you receive? If you cannot answer this question in advance you have not planned your research carefully enough and are wasting both your t me and that of the people who are to be studied.

When viewed from the perspective of what must be asked in order to measure the variables in this study, the construction of a questionnaire (or interview schedule) becomes fairly straightforward. It is hardly necessary to say that a short questionnaire has greater likelihood of being answered and is easier to analyse than a cumbersome long one. Identify what questions must be asked in order to measure a variable adequately. Discard the rest.

It is important to realize that most hypotheses and research objectives can be researched using more than one technique of data gathering. For example, the observational study of infant growth and development discussed earlier in this chapter could also have used a questionnaire or interview technique. If you were to distribute a data recording form similar to the one on p. 71 to the mothers of a number of infants, that form becomes a questionnaire. You would have to provide some instructions about how often to record the information and in what circumstances. None the less, what was a data recording form in the hands of a researcher could become a questionnaire for someone else to fill in.

Similarly, the study could have been done using interview techniques. The same data recording form would be used but the interviewer would visit, or telephone, the parent of the baby and ask, 'How much does your baby weigh today?', 'How long is your baby today?' In this case the researcher records the information on the data recording form. The researcher, of course, will maintain a separate form for each baby.

Let us take another example. Remember this hypothesis:

The more a student studies, the better will be that student's academic performance.

One of the operational forms of this hypothesis developed in Chapter 4 was:

The more hours spent in revision, the better will be a student's examination result.

This hypothesis was diagrammed:

You have been assigned to do a little research related
to this hypothesis. How are you going to measure the
variables? The problem is fairly straightforward in this
case. You can count hours easily and the examination results
can be recorded. You need to have a record for each student
involved, of two things and only two things—the number
of hours spent in revision and that student's examination
result.

Presume that a group of students are to have a history
examination in a month's time. You could ask each student to
keep a record of the time spent revising for that exam. Then get
each student's examination results. One way of doing this would
be to give each student a mini-questionnaire such as the one
that follows on p. 82.

This questionnaire measures the variable, hours spent
in revision, by asking each student to keep a record.
It presumes that students will be honest in reporting both
the time spent in revision and their examination results.
An alternative procedure would be to obtain a copy of the
examination results yourself and you could then collect the
questionnaires at the time of the examination. One problem
of using questionnaires is that you depend on the honesty
of the respondents. Sometimes this difficulty can be overcome
by allowing the respondents to complete the questionnaire
anonymously.

Once you have collected all the questionnaires you may wish
to use a form to summarize your data. In this case you have
data on two variables, time spent in revision and examination
result, for each of a certain number of students. Using a form
like the one on p. 83 may be useful to summarize and organize
your data. It will be particularly helpful when the time comes to
analyse your data. This summarization form preserves all the
information required by this study in a form useful for later
analysis.

As part of my course work I have to undertake a small scale research project and I would be most grateful for your help. I am studying the relationship between time spent in revision and examination results and I would like you to keep an account of the time you spend in revising history.

Student name: _____

	hrs	mins	hrs	mins
April		April		
8	_____	23	_____	
9	_____	24	_____	
10	_____	25	_____	
11	_____	26	_____	
12	_____	27	_____	
13	_____	28	_____	
14	_____	29	_____	
15	_____	30	_____	
16	_____	May	_____	
17	_____	1	_____	
18	_____	2	_____	
19	_____	3	_____	
20	_____	4	_____	
21	_____	5	_____	
22	_____	6	_____	
		7	_____	

Total time spent in revision:_____

After the examination place your result in this blank:

Examination result in history: _____%

Please return the questionnaire to me:
　　　　　　Harry Doolittle
　　　　　　Social Studies Office

Thank you for your help.

Figure 5.4 Questionnaire on time spent in revision

A suggested data summarization form

Student name or number	Hours spent in revision	Examination result

Here are some helpful hints for writing questionnaires which ask the respondent questions of fact.

1 Clarify exactly what it is you want to know. It is also important to ask yourself why you are asking the question. How does this question relate to your hypothesis?
2 In normal research, there are some basic questions asked. They are often referred to as 'face-sheet' variables, or questions, because they often appear on the front pages of the questionnaire. These questions request information about the respondent's age, sex, religion, marital status, education, income, and number of children. We are not

suggesting that all of these questions are necessary or useful for student projects. You should only ask those that are directly related to your project.

3 When asking a question of fact make sure that the question is clear and elicits a simple response of fact and not one of evaluation as well. Rather than asking a mother how she feels about the amount of television her child watches, a question such as, 'How many hours did your child spend watching television last night?' will provide a clear and simple factual answer.

4 Make sure the question is addressed to the right person. A mother may be able to tell you how many hours her child spent watching television. However, if you want the child's reaction to the programmes, it may be better to ask the child.

5 If you are asking a question about how much or how often, give a clear indication of the kind of response you want.

   How much time per week do you spend watching television? (in hours) _____

   How often do you watch the news? Tick one.

   once a day _____, three times per week _____, once a week _____, never _____

   Responses like often, frequently, most of the time, are too vague as they mean very different things to different people.

6 Be sure that respondents will be willing to answer the question. Deeply personal questions, or offensively worded questions, or questions that ask respondents to tell secrets or unpleasant information about themselves or others are not likely to be answered. For example, respondents are often uncomfortable about revealing their income.

7 Be direct and simple when asking questions. Spell out even commonly used initials so that there is no confusion (for example, Campaign for Nuclear Disarmament, not CND).

8 Avoid asking questions that raise more than one issue. For example, do not ask: 'Do you think the government should ban the closed shop because trade unions are bad for the economy?' This question raises too many issues. Someone might agree with the first part but not the second. Rewrite this as two questions which would give you clearer information about the respondent's position.

9 Try not to use colourful or emotive language in writing questions. Here is an example of a loaded question: 'Do you

agree that drunken drivers are a menace to society?' This is an emotively written question and should be written in a more balanced way.

Penalties for drunken driving should be increased.
Do you agree? _____ ?
disagree _____ ?

10 Do not word questions in such a way that the respondent is placed in an impossible position. For example, 'Have you stopped beating your wife?' or 'When did you stop poisoning your husband?' or 'When did you stop hating immigrants?'

11 It is always a good idea to test your questionnaire. Give it to some people who are not in your sample but are like the people you plan to study. Listen to what they say about the questions and in response to the questions. This will help to ensure that your questionnaire gives you the information you want.

The questionnaires examined to this point have been designed to gather *facts* from the respondent. How much does your baby weigh today? How long have you studied? What was your result on the history examination? Questionnaires and interviews are often also used to assess the respondent's attitudes, values, beliefs, or opinions. The construction of a questionnaire to measure opinions, attitudes, beliefs, and values is much more complex than simply asking questions of fact. Consider the following hypothesis:

Boys who have gone to single-sex schools are more sexist in their attitudes toward women than boys who have attended co-educational schools.

The concepts involved in this hypothesis are:

• socialization context
• sex role stereotyping

The variables are:

• independent variable — single-sex v. co-educational socialization context
• dependent variable — sexist attitudes

A questionnaire designed to test for sexist
attitudes among school-age boys

Name/identification number: _____

School: _____

Teacher: _____

Date: _____

1 Have the schools you have attended since you began school been (tick one):
  _____ a co-educational
  _____ b single sex
  _____ c both (co-educational and single-sex schools)?
	Do not write in this area
	 1

2 Please indicate your agreement or
disagreement with the following statements
by circling the response that most nearly
coincides with your own.

SA = Strongly Agree; A = Agree; U = Uncertain;
D = Disagree; SD = Strongly Disagree

a A woman would never make a good judge.	SA A U D SD	a
b Women are not as good at sport as men.	SA A U D SD	b
c Women should be encouraged to seek leadership positions.	SA A U D SD	c
d Men should not have to do any washing up.	SA A U D SD	d
e Men should be left to make money decisions.	SA A U D SD	e
		Total

A Likert scale on a questionnaire

The independent variable is easy to measure. Any boy either was or was not educated in a co-educational context. Boys who have had part of their education in each context can either be retained in a third category (mixed) or eliminated from the study. In this case the independent variable is a categorical variable. Respondents are placed in the appropriate category by their answer to a single question regarding their education. One of the first questions to be included in either an interview schedule or a questionnaire designed to measure this variable would be:

Have the schools you have attended from the time you began school till now been (tick one):
_____ a co-educational
_____ b single sex
_____ c both (co-educational and single-sex schools)?

Now comes the more difficult part. How do you propose to measure the dependent variable — sexist attitudes? This is a very complex variable. In general, sexism refers to the idea that one sex is in some way inferior or superior to the other. Simply to ask 'Are you sexist?' would only measure the respondent's self-perception. While this might be interesting in itself, the dependent variable is sexist attitudes not self-perception. What is required is a series of questions or statements designed to evoke reactions from the respondents, which taken together provide an indication of the respondent's sexist attitudes. While there are other kinds of scales, the additive scale is one of the easiest to construct and analyse. In this case the respondent is presented with a series of short statements and is asked to agree or disagree with each statement. The questionnaire on p. 86 is an example.

Why is this called a scale? It is a device to measure variation in an attitude. Its values range between two points and all respondents can be placed on that scale according to their responses to the questionnaire. It is an attitude scale. It is called a Likert scale after the person who invented it. In a Likert scale the respondent is asked to indicate agreement or disagreement with a series of short statements on a given (usually five-point) range of responses.

How does a Likert scale work? The responses are turned into a numerical scale by assigning numerical values to each of the responses and summing up the results. The scale can be made to run from a low number indicating a low degree of sexism to a

high number indicating a high degree of sexism by assigning
low numerical values to those responses indicating non-
sexist responses and high values to sexist responses. In the
example on p. 86, agreement with statements a, b, d, and e
indicates a sexist attitude; so does disagreement with c. The
numerical values assigned to each response in this case
would be:

For a, b, d, e: SA = 5
                    A = 4
                    U = 3
                    D = 2
                    SD = 1

For c: SA = 1
                    A = 2
                    U = 3
                    D = 4
                    SD = 5

The highest numerical value on this scale would be 25. To get
25 a respondent would have to indicate strong agreement with
items a, b, d, e, and strong disagreement with item c. If this
scale accurately measures sexist attitudes, such a person would
be sexist indeed. The lowest score on this scale would be 5. To
get a score of 5 a respondent would have to indicate strong
disagreement with items a, b, d, e, and strong agreement with
item c. Respondents who failed to answer all of the items would
have to be eliminated from the analysis. By adding the
numerical equivalents to each response the respondent's total
score can be calculated. Each respondent will have a score
between 5 and 25.

If you were satisfied that responses to the statements you
used gave an adequate indication of whether or not a person
held sexist attitudes, this scale would be all you would need
to test the hypothesis above. You have a measure for each
variable. The measure for the dependent variable is an attitude
scale. The measure for the independent variable is provided
by a single question related to the respondent's schooling.
If you were to use a data summarization sheet it might look
like this:

Data summarization sheet for a study of sexist
attitudes among boys in secondary school

Name or identification number	Type of schooling	Score on sexism scale

The shorter your questionnaire, the fewer extraneous items
included, the more likely is it to work. You need measures only
for those variables you are studying. It may be intriguing to ask
other questions, but they are not relevant to your study. For
example, it may have occurred to you that other questions could
be included in the above study on sexism. You might have
wanted to know such things as:

Does the boy's mother work?
Has the boy any sisters?
What does the boy's religion say about this?
Have all the boy's teachers been male or female?

While they are useful questions in themselves, due to the
limitations of time, energy, and the necessity to focus the study,
type of educational context was used as the sole independent
variable. Questions dealing with other issues were not raised.
The fact that you considered these factors to be potentially
relevant, but were not able to include them in your study,
should be noted in the limitations to your study.

Scales like the one above can be developed for nearly
everything. There are some basic rules which should be
followed. In making these suggestions we will state the ideal for
normal research and suggest some compromises which will be
acceptable for student projects. It is important to know what

would be done normally. It is also important to keep student projects manageable so that skills can be learned.

Suggestions for scale construction

1 The usual procedure is to begin with literally hundreds of suggested items and, through testing and critical feedback, narrow the number to between twenty and fifty. Student projects using Likert-type scale items should try to have fifteen items.
2 Each item should state one thing clearly. Here are some examples of what not to do. The following items have more than one key element:

- Women are brighter and better behaved than men.
- Men should not do washing up and women should not keep the cheque book.
- Men are stronger but women are more spiritual.

It would be much better if each item were split.

- Women are brighter than men.
- Women are better behaved than men.
- Men should not do washing up.
- Women should not keep the cheque book.
- Men are stronger than women.
- Women are more spiritual than men.

3 For a group of items to constitute a scale, each item must be related to a single theme. Each item should pick up a different aspect of, or slant on, the theme. For example, the items listed above all relate to the theme of attitudes towards the abilities of males and females. It would add a totally different dimension to the scale to add items on age difference or ethnic difference.
4 Response categories must be selected very carefully. They must be in one dimension and provide responses across the whole range of the dimension. While research is done using a wide variety of numbers of response categories, several conventions have emerged. The five-point Likert-type response category is most frequently used. These response categories are:

strongly agree   agree   undecided   disagree   strongly disagree

5 The more specific the response categories, the more accurate and precise the information that will be provided. For example:

Britain should have nuclear armaments	Strongly agree	Agree	Uncertain	Disagree	Strongly disagree
How often do you go to church?	Never	Once a year	Monthly	Weekly	Daily
How long did you study for this quiz?	Two hours	One hour	Half-hour	Quarter-hour	Not at all

Following is an example of what not to do. Read the item and the responses and ask yourself, 'What is wrong here?'

I find myself having to repress violent anti-social behaviour:

Almost all the time   Frequently   Often   With great effort
With considerable effort   With substantial effort

Have you identified the fact that the response categories cover two dimensions, frequency and intensity? Secondly, they provide for only one side of the response. 'Sometimes', 'hardly ever', and 'never' are not provided as possible response categories, nor are 'with ease', 'with no effort', etc.

One way to go about item selection is to produce a long list of items. Two processes of sifting can go on. First, go over the list with some friends to eliminate or rewrite inappropriate items. Secondly, give the whole list to a group of people very much like those for whom the questionnaire or interview is being designed. Talk to them afterwards about what you are trying to measure. They may have useful suggestions.

Try the following exercise to gain more experience in constructing an attitude scale to measure an attitude. Let us suppose that you have been asked to do a study related to nuclear disarmament. Your dependent variable is attitude towards nuclear disarmament. Assignment: Construct a five-item scale measuring attitude towards nuclear disarmament. Remember that you must not only write the items but also decide what range of responses to have. Once you have done that you will be able to specify what the highest and lowest possible scores are.

Now ask yourself:

1 How did I measure my dependent variable? How did
  I measure attitude towards nuclear disarmament? List the
  items.
2 What range of responses do I want to have?

  a Simple agree/disagree or a broader range?
  b Will I include a neutral position, or will I force the
    respondent to make a choice?

3 Will all the statements be positive or negative or will I vary
  the polarity of response? Compare the following examples:

  a There is no situation in which   SA A U D SD
    nuclear war is justified.
  b Cruise missiles should be removed   SA A U D SD
    from Britain.
  c Nuclear powered ships should be   SA A U D SD
    allowed to use our ports.
  d The development of nuclear-free   SA A U D SD
    areas is a waste of time.

Agreement with a and b would be taken to indicate an 'anti-
nuclear' response. However, agreement with c and d would
not indicate an anti-nuclear response. In this set of statements
the polarity of response is reversed. This is also true of the
set of statements designed to measure sexist attitudes
presented earlier. It is usually better to vary the response
pattern in this way. This prevents people from getting into
the habit of checking the same column. It helps to keep
respondents awake and thinking.

4 What is the highest possible score on the scale constructed
  from the items you listed above for Question 1? What is the
  lowest? This will depend on the number of items you have and
  the number of response categories you used. If you had five
  items and five response categories (SA A U D SD) then the
  highest possible score would be 25, and the lowest would be 5.
    Here is how the highest and lowest possible scores are
  calculated for the scale formed by responses to the four items
  relating to nuclear disarmament listed in Question 3 above.
    Let us say that you wanted your scale values to run from
  high (indicating strong pro-nuclear-disarmament attitudes) to
  low (indicating low pro-nuclear-disarmament attitudes). In this
  case the numerical values assigned to each response would be
  as follows:

For a and b   SA   A   U   D   SD
                  5   4   3   2   1

for c and d   SA   A   U   D   SD
                  1   2   3   4   5

The reason for this is that agreement with a and b indicates a pro-nuclear-disarmament position, while *dis*agreement with c and d does. When the polarity of response is reversed, so is the numerical value assigned to the response categories. In this case the highest possible score would be given to the person who made which responses? What is the highest possible score? What is the lowest?

A scale of values can be developed along which respondents can be positioned on the basis of their response to items on a questionnaire, or an interview schedule. The responses are taken as indicators of the person's attitude, or belief, or value. The scale is a device for measuring variation in a person's commitment to the attitude, or the strength with which it is held. While there are many complicated issues in the measurement of attitudes, values, and beliefs, you should now be familiar with the basic logic.

There is still one more form of questionnaire to be considered. This form involves ranking options. Ranking is often used in research into values and preferences. Voters are often asked to rank candidates. Respondents can be asked to rank options, candidates, preferences, commodities, or values. Ranking forces the respondent to make careful discrimination among the options. It is important that all the options be of the same kind. Here is an example:

Rank the following values from most (1) to least (7) in terms of their importance to you:

loyalty	_____	independence	_____
excitement	_____	equality	_____
peace	_____	creativity	_____
security	_____		

Here is another example:

Rank the following qualities from most (1) to least (8) in terms
of how you would assess a potential marriage partner:

_____ appearance		_____ sensitivity
_____ honesty		_____ ability to learn
_____ integrity		_____ money
_____ sense of humour		_____ religiosity
		_____ flexibility

Respondents, or groups of respondents, can be compared in
terms of the way they ranked options. For example, you might
find that a group of girls on average ranked sensitivity higher
than appearance, while a group of boys on average ranked a
sense of humour above flexibility. Ranking options provides
another way of measuring respondents' values and preferences.

The questionnaire and the interview schedule are data
gathering techniques by which a researcher can measure the
variables under study. In these techniques, questions are asked
in order to gain information from the respondent. This
information can be factual. How did you vote? How old are
you? How much does your baby weigh? Or questions may be
asked in order to determine a person's attitudes, beliefs, or
values.

Examining records to measure variables

The third common data gathering technique is to measure
variables by using the information kept in records, or official
reports of organizations, government agencies, or persons.
Possibly the most familiar example of this kind of data is the
Census. Records are kept on marriages, divorces, deaths, and
certain kinds of financial transactions. Organizations keep
records. Hospitals keep records of admissions and discharges,
types of surgery performed, and amount of use of their
facilities. Some churches keep records of number of members,
marriages, baptisms, amount of money received and paid.
Schools keep records of numbers of students, student–teacher
ratios, and what subjects were taught.

The basic problem with using recorded information to
measure a variable is gaining access to the information. Most
libraries will contain the *Guide to Official Statistics* published
by HMSO. As its title implies, this gives the source of a wide

range of statistics collected by the government. Other sources of information are reference books such as *Whitaker's Almanack* and the year-books or annual reports of firms and organizations.

The second problem is that the statistics reported are often not exactly what you want. They may be for England and Wales when you want data for the UK as a whole. And information may be collected in one way in 1980 and in another in 1985, making comparisons difficult. Despite the difficulties, a huge amount of information on social and economic matters is available from published sources. If you are in an institution with a good library, the publications should be available there; if not you may have to try the public library in a large town. If there is a university or polytechnic in the area it is worth a visit because most make their facilities (though not loans) available to non-members. The best course is to ask a librarian.

Content analysis

Content analysis is a different way to examine records or documents or publications. Content analysis is very much like an observation study. In a content analysis a checklist is developed to count how frequently certain ideas, words, phrases, images, or scenes appear. It is like an observation study, but what is being observed is a text, or a film or television programme.

One study of the perception of the aged in our society involved the researchers' watching a night's television. What was to be observed? The roles that were played by the elderly in television commercials. Another approach required that the researcher deduce the needs of the elderly on the basis of advertisements aimed at the elderly.

The procedure for a content analysis of television or radio programmes follows the same lines as an observation study. The possibility of recording the programme allows the researcher to go back over the material several times to complete and check the accuracy of the content analysis. It provides an opportunity for several people to do a content analysis of the same material, and it helps them examine the material to see what things can be observed and counted. The steps for preparing a content analysis of television or radio material are therefore:

1 Clarify and narrow your hypothesis or research objective. What are the concepts involved?

2 Identify variables related to the concepts under study. This may involve watching some television programmes or listening to radio programmes to become familiar with what there is to be observed.
3 Devise a way to measure the variables. Develop a checklist to count how often the things you selected to observe appear, e.g. number of advertisements featuring the elderly; number of advertisements in which women play roles of authority.
4 Decide what programmes to examine, or during what period of time you will observe the radio or television. This will involve deciding whether your unit of analysis is the time period (e.g. two hours of Wednesday night prime time television), or a specific programme, or a number of advertisements over a period of time (e.g. the first ten advertisements screened after 6 p.m. on Channel 4 on Friday nights).
5 Devise a data summarization sheet.
6 Collect your data by doing the observations you propose.
7 Summarize the results on the data summarization form.

The content analysis of published material

Published material is a storehouse of material for content analysis. Magazines, periodicals, books, novels, textbooks, all can be subjected to content analysis. The logic of research using content analysis of published material is the same as the logic of other kinds of research. The first step is to clarify your hypothesis or research objective. Once the concepts under study have been identified, variables can be selected that are related to the concepts. Then the problem of how to measure and record variation in the variables can be tackled. Once measurement problems are settled, the units of measure in which to report findings can be decided. Remember this flow:

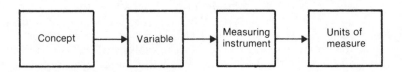

This same flow of issues occurs in designing research using the content of written material. Presume that you are interested in the area of sex-role stereotyping. You are interested in the origin of sex-role stereotypes—where do they come from? One possible source would be children's story-books. This might lead you to ask whether there has been a change in the amount of sex-role stereotyping in children's books. How could you measure change in the amount of sex-role stereotyping over a number of years?

One possible way would be to examine the reading material used to teach reading to children in infant departments. What are infants reading today compared with twenty years ago? To do this you would need access to the readers used twenty years ago and the readers used now. Secondly you need to develop a set of indicators of sexism. What roles do girls and boys play? What roles do men and women play? What activities characterize each sex? Do the illustrations promote sex-role stereotyping? Once you have begun to identify countable features of these readers you can devise a checklist on sex-role stereotyping in first-stage readers.

Or you might devise a set of questions to put to each set of readers like the one below:

	Place tick in appropriate column				
	Always	**In over half the stories**	**Half and half**	**In less than half the stories**	**Never**
1 Are boys shown to dominate girls?					
2 Are girls shown to win against boys?					
3 Is unisex clothing used?					
4 Are women shown in traditionally male roles? e.g. a female physician or a female priest					
5 Does a male ask a female for help or directions or information?					
6 Are females shown to be helpless?					

In this way a scale of sex-role stereotyping in literature can be developed. By applying it to literature from different times, changes can be observed and systematic comparisons made.

Here is another example of research using content analysis of published material. Since the Second World War an increasing proportion of married women has been employed. Has this movement into paid work outside the home had an impact on the publications directed at women? The hypothesis could be:

As the proportion of women who are employed out of the home increases there will be an increase in the attention paid to working women in the publications aimed at women.

This can be diagrammed:

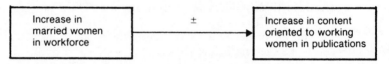

Since we know there has been an increase in the proportion of married women who are employed we only need to find variables to provide an indication of change in the dependent concept—change in content of material published for women. Several approaches are possible.

First, the number of magazines published for women may have changed from 1947 to the present. Are there more or less now? Are some of the new ones directed mainly at employed married women? You might gain help from your library on the number and kind of women's magazines that have come and gone since 1947.

A second approach would be to select one title that has been published consistently over a long period of time, for example *Woman's Own* or *Vogue*. It would be interesting to see if the number of articles which appeal to working women, or address the problems faced by working women, has changed. Here you must decide what to count. Do you count articles, or the number of pages? Do you take just one issue or a year of issues? It would be better to deal with more than one issue in each year in case the issue you chose for a given year is atypical. You might take one volume from each month. The results would be reported as the number of articles or pages per year appealing to working women.

A third approach would be to see if the magazine's attitude to the idea of married women working has changed. It is possible, for example, that *Woman's Own* has devoted roughly the same number of articles or pages or proportion of space to the subject of employed married women, but that it has shifted from disapproval to approval. This would require not only the counting of articles or pages devoted to the subject but deciding whether each was favourable, unfavourable, or neutral. Your record of research might look like this:

A record sheet for a content analysis of articles dealing with employed married women

Magazine: _____ Issue: _____

Year: _____ Total pages:_____

Total no. of articles: _____

Title of article	Number of pages	Orientation expressed
Total no. of articles	Total no. of pages	

Let us say that twelve issues each for the years 1950 and 1985 were read. There would be twenty-four record sheets; one for each issue. The analysis would be by year.

Data summary sheet for content analysis

	1950	1985
Total pages		
Number of pages devoted to employed married women		
Proportion of total pages devoted to employed married women		
Total number of articles		
Number of articles devoted to employed married women		
Proportion of articles devoted to employed married women		

The classification of the content of the articles as favourable, unfavourable, or neutral would proceed on similar lines. There might be additional categories that would need to be introduced after all the material was read.

Content analysis can be fun. Popular music, movies, and magazines are interesting to analyse. Before you begin content analysis refer to the following checklist:

Preparation for research using content analysis to collect data

1 Clarify the hypothesis. What concepts are involved?
2 What variables can be used to indicate change in or differences between the concepts?
3 How can this variable be measured using content analysis? What is to be counted—pages, words, articles, pictures, or something else? Devise a record sheet for recording your data.
4 In what units are the results to be reported—pages per issue, words per year, articles per week, or something else? Devise a data summarization sheet for reporting your data.

Validity

At the end of the last chapter the problem of validity was discussed. The problem of validity is concerned with how accurately a variable fits a concept. Does the variable selected adequately reflect what is important about the concept? Most people would accept changes in size as a valid indicator of growth in babies, but some concepts are more difficult to pin down. You may not have been fully satisfied with the variables selected in the examples used in this chapter. You may have questioned the validity of some of the variables. For example, is talking to a neighbour a valid indicator of classroom behaviour? Is a test in history a valid way to test a student's grasp of historical material? While some variables are so invalid as indicators they should not be used, most variables that are used can be questioned in one way or another. These questions are best included in the limitations to the study. If a variable is shown to lack absolute validity, say so in the limitations to the study section of the report.

The problem of validity is most acute in the construction of questionnaires or interview schedules to 'measure' a person's attitudes, or beliefs, or values. For example, it is necessary to ask whether the items used to measure variation in a person's attitudes to nuclear disarmament are valid. On reflection, only one deals with nuclear war. The others deal with the use of nuclear material in other ways. It is very possible for someone who is very much in favour of nuclear disarmament to be in favour of the peaceful use of nuclear material for the generation of power. The items do not focus clearly on the variable to be measured. They lack validity.

What of the items designed to measure sexist attitudes in schoolboys? Are they valid? Should there be some note included in a report of that study indicating that the researcher is aware of the limitations of the measures selected to indicate change or variation in the variables under consideration?

It is important to be aware of the problems of validity. In professional research a great deal of time and effort is spent ensuring validity. As a student there are things that you can do too. In addition to being very careful in your construction of measuring devices, record sheets, questionnaires, and checklists, you can ask your friends and your teacher to comment on your measures. This may help to increase their validity. Moreover, you can pre-test scales using individuals known to exhibit extremes of the dimensions you are trying to measure. For example, what would it mean for the validity of your scale if someone whom you knew to be very sexist got a low score on a sexism scale which you had devised? Clearly, you would have to rework your scale! It is very important to *pre*-test your research instrument to ensure that it is working properly before actually doing your research.

Reliability

The question of reliability is different from the question of validity. When someone asks if a measure is reliable, they are asking whether different researchers using the same measuring device would get the same results when measuring the same event. For example, will a group of ten students who weigh the same baby one after another record the same weight? Is a baby-weighing scale reliable? This may depend on how wriggly the baby is. But that is a legitimate part of the problem. The basic question is whether the measurement device employed provides the same results when repeated. This is called test-retest reliability.

The reliability of observation techniques is often questioned. Will a group of observers report the same observations? This is also a problem in content analysis. Will several people agree that article X dealt with a topic related to the needs of working married women? Will they agree that it took a positive orientation? The more agreement there is in coding observations on content analysis the more reliable is the instrument.

A valuable asset of recorded or published materials is that you can go back over the material. Where there are differences it is possible to sort them out with those who are evaluating the material. Was the comment made by the daughter ignored, or was it ridiculed? If you are unsure, you can go back to that bit of the tape and check. The challenge to the reliability of a measure is that different researchers using the same measure may record different results.

Questions of reliability refer to problems in the accuracy of the measuring device. Questions of validity refer to the appropriateness of the measuring device. It is important for you to be aware of each of these kinds of problem. It is appropriate to include questions about validity and reliability in any discussion of the limitations of your research.

Summary

Once you have clarified your hypothesis and selected variables for study, the issue of measurement must be considered. Three basic techniques for measuring variables have been discussed: observation techniques, questionnaire or interview schedules, and content analysis. The importance of developing systematic data recording forms and data summarization forms has been emphasized. The fact that one collects data to measure variables in a hypothesis is the major emphasis of this chapter. Data gathering is done to measure variables one has clarified beforehand.

Questions for review

1 What are the basic steps in preparing to do research involving observation as a data gathering technique?
2 What is the purpose of a checklist for observation?
3 What is the purpose of a data summarization sheet?
4 What are the basic steps in preparing research involving the use of a questionnaire or interview schedule?
5 What is the difference between an interview schedule and a questionnaire?
6 How do you determine the highest and lowest possible scores on a scale framed by responses to items designed to measure a respondent's attitudes, values, or beliefs?
7 What does it mean to reverse the polarity of response for an item? What impact does this have on the way the responses are scored for scale construction?
8 What are the steps involved in preparing to do research involving the use of content analysis?
9 What is the problem of validity?
10 What is the problem of reliability?

6

Selecting a research design

Do you remember our definition of a hypothesis? A hypothesis is a statement which asserts a relationship between two or more concepts. A hypothesis is developed in order to focus the aim of research. The same is true of a research objective. It is developed to guide the research undertaken. When you are actually doing some research it can be very helpful to keep your hypothesis on a card that you can see. Your research will be done to test the hypothesis or to meet the objective set.

How does the hypothesis guide the research? The hypothesis claims that there there is a relationship between X and Y. Research is undertaken to determine whether there is evidence to support this claim. In order to carry out the research two basic things must be done. Firstly the concepts in the hypothesis must be defined in such a way that they can be measured. In the last two chapters we have learned how to select variables that relate to the concepts in our hypothesis and how to devise ways of measuring the variables we have selected. However, research requires more than the measurement of the concepts in a hypothesis.

The second requirement for testing a hypothesis is to find some indication that the relationship it states actually exists. Measuring X and Y is one thing. Finding an indication that X and Y are related is another. While the *measurement* of concepts is taken care of by operational definitions of the concepts in the

hypothesis, the relationship between X and Y is assessed by the research design.
Let us look at our diagram of a hypothesis again.

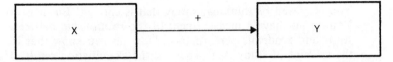

This hypothesis states that a change in X will produce a change in Y and that the nature of the relationship between X and Y is such that an increase in X will produce an increase in Y. One of the hypotheses we have been using as an example states:

The more a student studies, the better will be that student's academic performance.

The conceptual form of this hypothesis was diagrammed:

A number of variables for each of the concepts was identified. (If you cannot remember them, turn back to the beginning of Chapter 4 to refresh your memory.) The variable selected as related to the concept study was 'number of hours spent in revision'. The variable taken to be associated with academic performance was 'exam results'. Having done this the hypothesis can be restated in its variable form as follows:

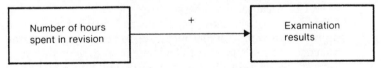

In Chapter 5 we went on to devise measures for each of the variables in this hypothesis. Can you remember them? Students were asked to keep an account of the time they spent revising for a specific history test. They were also asked to record the result that they received in the history examination. The operational definition of the hypothesis, the statement of the hypothesis as a specified relationship between measures, would be as follows:

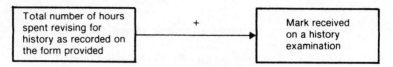

You may well be thinking, surely that is enough! But it is not. You do not have a measurement of the *relationship* between study and academic performance. How do you know that it was the amount of study that produced the examination result? How do you know that a change in the independent variable produced a change in the dependent variable?

What kinds of relationships can there be among variables? There are three basic types:

1 The variables are not related.
2 The variables are related.
3 The variables are causally related, that is, a change in one variable will produce a change in the other variable.

It is relatively easy to determine whether two variables are related. It is more difficult to determine that X causes Y. In order to establish that two variables are causally related it is necessary to show that:

1 X and Y are related.
2 That changes in X precede changes in Y.
3 That all other variables which might produce the changes in Y are controlled.

As we shall see, the experimental research design is the only design truly adequate for testing a causal hypothesis. Given that an experimental design is not always possible or practical or permissible, other designs are used to approximate an experimental design or to provide some information relevant to the test of a causal hypothesis.

This is one of the most important and difficult parts of doing empirical research. Finding measures for concepts is a great challenge. The second great challenge is to design ways to discover the relationship between variables. You may feel certain that an increase in study will produce an increase in academic performance. But how do you *prove* that these concepts are related in this way? How do you design your research to answer this question?

The basic types of research design can be divided into five types. The type you select will depend on the hypothesis or research objective you have set for yourself. Each type of research design answers a different question. In this chapter we will examine each of these types of research design. We will use the example of designing a piece of research to examine the relationship between study and academic performance. By using one hypothesis in describing each type of research design it should become clear that each type of design can provide some evidence related to a hypothesis. While one design may be more desirable than another for certain hypotheses, each design makes a particular contribution.

One way to become familiar with the logic of research design is to understand that each type of research design asks a different kind of question. The basic types of research design can be grouped according to five different questions.

1 What is happening?
   What are the basic variables? Are X and Y related?
2 Has there been a change?
   Does the relationship between X and Y change when measured at two different times?
3 Is Group A different from Group B?
   Is the relationship between X and Y in Group A different from their relationship in Group B?
4 Has there been a difference between Group A and Group B over time?
   Has there been a change in the relationship between X and Y in Group A as compared with Group B when measured at different times?
5 Why are Groups A and B different?
   Is a change in the value of X associated with a change in the value of Y in Group A while in Group B no change in X is associated with no change in Y?

We will develop each design in detail so that you can see the value and limitations of each.

1   The case study

The case study can answer the question, 'What is going on?' In a case study, a single case (hence the name) is studied for a period of time and the results recorded. A case study may be of one person, one group, one family, one classroom, one town, one nation. The aim of the case study is description. What is going on? Is there a relationship between X and Y? It is also possible to do a case study focusing on one variable. The key element in a case study is that one group is focused on and that no comparison with another group is made.

The term 'case study' is used in several ways by people who discuss research design. Some limit the use of the term to an *exploratory study* in which no hypothesis is tested. For example, you might be interested in the factors a particular family or group of families takes into consideration when planning meals. You simply want to know what is going on. You are not testing a hypothesis. You are not comparing one group of families with another. An observation study of one family or group of families would provide adequate data for a research objective such as 'What factors are considered by the person(s) in charge of meal planning in a (group of) household(s)?' The result would be a list of factors.

When a case study is an exploratory study, one of the purposes of the research may be to ascertain the relevant variables for a particular area of study. Such a study might also be done to help to formulate a hypothesis for later study. An exploratory study takes a very broad look at the phenomenon under study. Attention is not as focused as in a study to test a hypothesis. The purpose is to gather information, so that a description of what is going on can be made.

However, not all case studies are exploratory studies. Some case studies are done in order to provide an initial test of a hypothesis. The sort of hypothesis that can be tested by a case study could take this form: 'That there is a relationship between X and Y'. A causal relationship is not being tested since it is very difficult to rule out alternative explanations in a case study. There are times when it is useful to check to see if two variables show any relationship before going to the trouble of more rigorous testing.

Our key example concerns the relationship between study and academic performance. What data can a case study provide? It can tell whether in one instance there was a relationship between amount of study and academic performance. Is there any relationship between X and Y? The value in such a study is that if no relationship is found there may be little point in pursuing the more difficult kinds of research design required to test the hypothesis that the more a student studies the better will that student's academic performance be.

A case study designed to discover whether there is any relationship between study and academic performance might take this form. The questionnaire on time spent in revision developed in the last chapter would be given to a specific

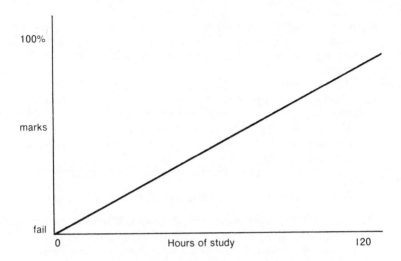

Figure 6.1 A sample graph of possible results from a case study

history class. The class is the case. The measurement is carried out once. The results are assessed once for one class and one examination. The data would then be analysed. While we will deal with data analysis in greater detail later, let us say that you discovered that amount of study time did positively relate to the marks achieved. Your graph might have looked like Figure 6.1.

What would your graph have looked like if you found that the amount of time spent studying related negatively to the marks achieved? What could you have concluded from this study if you had done it as described and obtained results like those in Figure 6.1? You could conclude that in the group of students examined there was a positive relationship between amount of study and academic performance as measured by the instrument devised. You could not conclude that amount of study caused the level of marks. You do not know whether it is true of some other groups of students or merely a fluke in this case. All you know is that in one case at one point in time this was the result. You also have no basis upon which to rule out alternative explanations. For example the students who studied longer might also have sat in the front of the room and paid better attention. What caused the differences in result, study or attention?

You might be prompted by your curiosity to test other factors or to compare the results of tests of other groups of students.

Knowing what happened in one case may prompt you to try other cases. Or it might persuade you to test whether it really was the amount of time spent in revision that produces the results.

Before going on to the next type of study, consider the following example. You are interested in the incomes and spending patterns of young people and a case study is one way in which this can be investigated to find out what is going on. You can do this by studying a particular group—say the top class in a primary school.

Your research objective for this case study might be:

To discover the incomes and spending patterns of top juniors.

To measure these concepts variables will have to be selected. For adults 'income' can be difficult to measure because it can include not only earnings but also interest and profits and can be calculated before or after tax. The problem is simpler for top juniors because pocket-money and presents can be used to measure income and information on these can be discovered by using a simple questionnaire. Spending is often less easy to measure because it is easy to forget what precisely we have spent our money on. The best method is to ask the children to keep a diary for a week as suggested in Figure 6.2.

Name _____ Age _____ Week beginning _____

Spending money received _____

Presents received _____

Spending day	Things bought	Cost
Sunday		
Monday		
Tuesday		
Wednesday		
Thursday		
Friday		
Saturday		

Figure 6.2 A diary to discover the income and spending patterns of top juniors

You may ask the children to complete the diary for a second week in case the first week was exceptional; for example, several children may have had birthdays which would distort the pattern.

You could use this data to find the average pocket-money and to answer questions such as 'Do boys receive more than girls?', 'Do the older children receive more?', 'What kinds of goods do the children spend most of their money on?'

The results can be presented as percentages as shown in Figure 6.3. The use of percentages makes it easier to compare the results for this class with those for other groups.

	Sweets	Comics	Toys	Records	Other
Percentage	40	10	5	15	30

Figure 6.3 Hypothetical percentages of spending patterns of top juniors

When carrying out case studies it is often advisable to undertake a pilot project first. This involves a practice run-through with a different, smaller group in order to iron out any snags. In this case for example a pilot project may show some deficiency in the design of the diary.

The case study is the basic building block of research design. In a case study a variable or set of variables is measured in one group (or individual) at one point in time. The other research designs involve studying in more than one group, or studying the same group at different times in order to make comparisons. In a sense each of the other research designs involves comparing the results of more than one case study in order to test a hypothesis. We will describe the design of the longitudinal study next.

2 The longitudinal study

The longitudinal research design involves two or more case studies of the same group with a period of time between each study. The basic question posed by a longitudinal study is, 'Has there been any change over a period of time?' In a very elementary sense the observation research described in the last chapter to measure the physical growth of a baby can be seen as a longitudinal study of one baby's growth. Measurement was carried out at weekly intervals, the results recorded and compared with previous results. Similarly, the case study just described could be extended into a longitudinal study. The same group could be asked for their incomes and spending patterns on several occasions either over a year or else, more ambitiously, over several years.

Longitudinal research designs sometimes include the use of official records or statistics. A longitudinal study of the birth rate could be done by finding out what the birth rate was in each of the last X years. Figure 9.17 on p. 192 gives longitudinal data on changes in the divorce rate in Britain. In this case, changes in one variable, divorce rate, are measured for one case, Britain, over three decades. The data needed for some longitudinal studies are available in official records. For example you could do a longitudinal study of the growth rate of your town or suburb and its relationship to the number of students attending the schools in the area over the last few years (depending on the age of the schools and the availability of records).

Another familiar form of the longitudinal study is the 'before and after study'. Some teachers give before and after tests in order to see if their lessons have had any effect on their students' knowledge. The study of the impact of diet on physical characteristics frequently takes a before and after longitudinal research design. 'He weighed 96 kg before following our strict diet and exercise regime and after only three months he weighed 80 kg.'

The longitudinal research design compares several measures of the same person, or group, or thing, over a period of time. It asks, 'Have there been any changes in variables measured over a period of time?' A longitudinal research design involving two measures of the same group over time can be diagrammed as follows:

Figure 6.4 A diagram of a longitudinal study involving two measures of group or individual A over time

Longitudinal research asks the question, 'Has there been any change in group or individual A between Time 1 and Time 2?'

Of course, additional points in time are possible. Remember the example of weighing and measuring a baby.

Returning to our example of the relationship between study and academic performance we can ask, what additional information would a longitudinal study provide? In the section on the case study we suggested that the result of the research was that amount of time spent in revision and the mark on a history test were positively related. The more time a student spent in revision, the better was that student's mark. One possible longitudinal study would be to repeat the same case study for the next history test to see whether the relationship continued to hold. This would help to find out whether the result in the case study had been simply a fluke. If it were found to hold again, our confidence in the finding and in the worth of the hypothesis would increase.

A study of student snack selections at a school tuckshop could be used to develop a longitudinal study. Details of sales could be obtained from those running the shop. Let us assume that 70 per cent of children's expenditure was for sweets (lollies, chocolates) and only 10 per cent of spending was on fruit. The teachers decided to try to improve the children's diet by giving lessons on nutrition. When this teaching was completed, the initial research could be repeated to see if there had been changes in the children's spending patterns.

What could the teachers conclude if the results looked like those in Figure 6.5? Would it be legitimate to conclude that the teaching was a success? Could the teachers conclude that as a result of the lessons there was a shift of student snack selections towards more fruit? No.

	Before	After
Sweets	70%	50%
Fruit	10%	30%
Other	20%	20%

Figure 6.5 Hypothetical results of a longitudinal study

The only conclusion legitimately drawn is that students were selecting more fruit. While it is likely that the lessons had some impact, only a Type 5 research design, an experimental design, can test whether it was the teaching that produced the results.

There may well have been other factors that caused the shift, which were quite unrelated to the lessons on selecting nutritious snacks. The stock at the tuckshop might have changed. The price of sweets might have gone up. The football coach might have told his team members to eat fruit not sweets or they would be off the team. Neither the simple case study nor the longitudinal study controlled these other factors. They are not adequate to rule out alternative explanations.

A longitudinal study asks, 'Has there been any change?' The answer is yes or no and some indication of how much. It cannot by itself identify and isolate the *cause* of the change. That requires an experimental research design.

To do a longitudinal study you:
1 Select variables relevant to the concepts under study.
2 Devise a way of measuring those variables.
3 Develop a data recording device.
4 Measure the same variables in the same way in one group (or for one person) at two or more times.

Such a study will enable you to determine whether there has been any change over a period of time.

3   The comparison

While the longitudinal research design involves the study of the same group through time, the *comparison* involves comparing one measure of two or more groups. The measures are ideally taken at the same time. The question addressed by a comparison study is, 'Are A and B different?'

The teachers concerned about student snack selection in the tuckshop might have been interested to find out whether there was any difference between children who had studied home economics and those who had not. To make this comparison the teacher would have to observe and record the selections made by two groups of students. It would be best if they could both be observed at the same time. The observation recording sheet might look like this:

	Group A	Group B
Sweets		
Fruit		
Other		

Figure 6.6 An observation recording form for a comparison study of snack selections made by two groups of students

Let us say that Group A are the home economics students and Group B the non home economics students. What could the teacher conclude if the results looked like those in Figure 6.7? She could conclude that, of the students observed, home economics students, on average, selected fewer sweets and more fruit than did non home economics students. The teacher might think that this difference was due to the nutrition education components in the home economics course. However, there is no way of telling this from the above study. The above study simply asks the question, 'Are these two groups of students different?' If the results in Figure 6.7 were obtained, the answer would be, yes. While we will deal with this issue in greater depth in the next chapter, it is important to remember that the findings of this study are limited to the students actually studied. The researcher cannot generalize further in this instance.

Information regarding the relationship between study and academic performance can be provided by a comparison study. It may have occurred to you that the relationship between amount of study and mark on the history exam held true for history but might not hold true for maths. One way to find out if subject matter made any difference in the relationship between amount of study and examination result would be to do the research designed above as a case study but for two classes, a maths class and a history class. The same type of record keeping form would be used, one for history and one for maths. The results of the two classes could be plotted on one graph similar to Figure 6.1 on p. 109.

What would be concluded if the results looked like those in Figure 6.8? Figure 6.8 shows a clear and positive relationship between the number of hours spent in revision and examination

	Home economics students	Non home economics students
Sweets	60%	70%
Fruit	30%	20%
Other	10%	10%

Figure 6.7 Hypothetical results of a comparison study of student snack selection

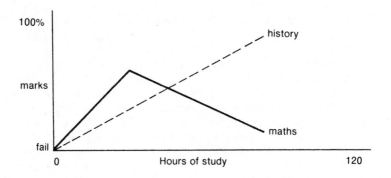

Figure 6.8 A sample graph of possible results from a comparison study

result in history. The same is not true for maths. In maths those that studied least and most received the lowest marks, while those who studied for an in-between amount of time received the highest marks. The researcher would conclude that the relationship between the amount of time spent in revision and examination result is different between Groups A and B. A and B are different.

What would be concluded if the results were like those in Figure 6.9? Be careful in reading this graph. Given these results the researcher would conclude that in the case of both history and maths the amount of time spent in revision was positively related to examination results. Given these results, the conclusion would be that Groups A and B were not different.

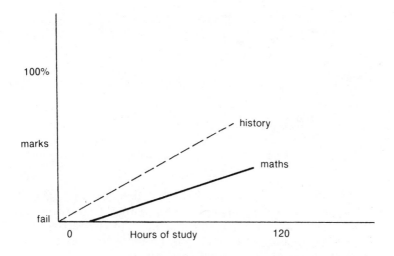

Figure 6.9 A sample graph of possible results from a comparison study

There are many times when a comparison study is as close as it is possible to get to an experiment. For example, take the hypothesis:

Females are more likely to do well at maths than males.

Which is the independent variable? The independent variable is gender—male v. female. This cannot be contested or manipulated as is required for an experiment. It is possible to compare two groups, one male and one female. In this instance the independent variable defines the groups being compared. The question becomes, can the difference between the two groups be attributed to the one factor known to be different? The answer is yes, so long as all other explanations are ruled out. If they are not, the answer is, perhaps.

In a comparison study two different groups are compared using the same measure of the same variables at or nearly at the same time. The comparison study can be diagrammed as follows:

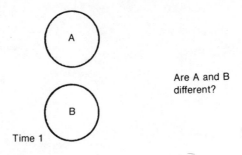

Figure 6.10 A diagram of a comparison study

A great deal of research is of the comparative type. Does Group A have the same birth-rate as Group B? Is there any difference between the political opinions of engineering students and those taking sociology? How do those who eat a vegetarian diet compare with those who also eat meat?

> To do a comparison study you:
> 1 Select variables related to the concepts under study.
> 2 Devise a way of measuring the variables.
> 3 Develop a data recording device.
> 4 Measure the same variables in the same way in two or more groups (or individuals) at the same or nearly the same time.

Such a study will enable you to determine whether there is any difference between the two groups.

4   The longitudinal comparison

We said earlier that the case study was in a sense the basic building block of research design. We have combined two case studies of the same group at two different times to produce a *longitudinal* study. Similarly by combining two case studies, each one of two groups at the same time, we produced the *comparison* study. When the comparison and the longitudinal types are combined the *longitudinal comparison* research design is produced. This type of research design asks the question, 'Are A and B different over a period of time?'

A good example of this type of research would be a study of two groups of babies. One group was bottle-fed and the other breast-fed. Each group was measured at the same interval—weekly for eight weeks beginning one week after birth. The observation recording device developed earlier would be used. Assume that Group A is bottle-fed and Group B breast-fed.

This study is longitudinal in that it involves a series of measures of the same variables in the same groups over time. It is a comparison because the two groups differ in a significant aspect. How might the data look? You have weight and length measure for each infant at weekly intervals. For the purpose of comparison between the two groups let us assume that you report the average weight gain each week. The following table might be used to present the results.

Average weight gain per week in grams

Week	1	2	3	4	5	6	7	8	Total
Group A	13	14	14	15	16	16	15	15	118
Group B	14	15	15	16	16	17	16	16	125

Figure 6.11 A table of possible results from a longitudinal comparison study of two groups of babies

Should results like those in Figure 6.11 have been the result, what conclusions could the researcher draw? The researcher could conclude only that Group B babies grew faster and more than Group A babies. In this hypothetical case the breast-fed babies grew faster and more than did the bottle-fed babies. While the difference in growth may be due to the difference in feeding, the researcher cannot be sure, since other possibly relevant factors have not been controlled.

The research into the relationship between amount of study and academic performance can be done using a longitudinal comparison type of research design. We will retain the comparison between a history class and a maths class. We will also use the same data recording form as before. As you may recall, in our last hypothetical research into this topic we discovered that there was a difference in the relationship between time spent in revision and examination result between maths and history. The question that can be asked is 'Does this difference persist through time?' By asking the two classes to keep a record of the time spent revising each subject before two exams a few months apart, a longitudinal comparison is achieved. We will have two measures for each of two groups at two different times. A diagram of this research design might look like Figure 6.12.

You may recall that our first comparison study of history and maths results looked like Figure 6.13.

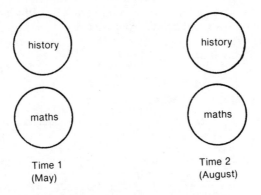

Figure 6.12 Diagram of a longitudinal comparison study of effect of amount of study on academic performance

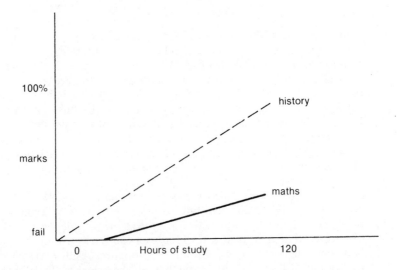

Figure 6.13 A sample graph of possible results from a longitudinal comparison study (first trial)

What conclusions were drawn on the basis of the data depicted in Figure 6.12? A longitudinal comparison essentially involves doing a second comparison study using the same measures as the first one to see if there has been any change between the two groups.

If the results of the second study were the same as the first, the conclusion would be that the difference between the two groups has persisted. The researcher might also be led towards the tentative conclusion that the difference might be due to something about the two subjects. On the other hand the results of the second part of this longitudinal comparison study might have looked like Figure 6.14.

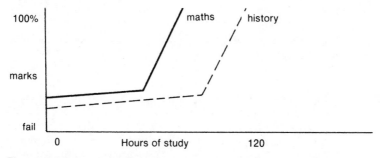

Figure 6.14 A sample graph of possible results from a longitudinal comparison study (second trial)

What conclusions could be drawn from these results? First, the differences between Groups A and B (history and maths in this study) have lessened. Secondly, the pattern for both subjects has changed. Have the students changed their study patterns? Were the examinations different? What has produced the change? That is still unknown. The longitudinal comparison research design does not provide adequate controls, nor does it give you the ability to manipulate the independent variable.

This same problem arises in the case of the home economics teacher who is concerned about student snack selection. Let us say that the teacher, after conducting the first comparison study between home economics and non home economics students, decided to put up posters in the tuckshop which promoted fruit as a health snack. After a few weeks the original comparison study is repeated. By repeating it, the original comparison study is transformed into a longitudinal comparison study.

What conclusions could the teacher draw from the following results?

	Home economics students		Non home economics students	
	May	**July**	**May**	**July**
Sweets	60%	40%	70%	50%
Fruit	30%	50%	20%	40%
Other	10%	10%	10%	10%

Figure 6.15 Hypothetical results of a longitudinal comparison study of student snack selection

Both groups have changed. Both groups shifted 20 percentage points in the direction of the greater consumption of fruit. The difference between the two groups has persisted. The home economics students are still more likely to select fruit than the non home economics students. However, it is impossible to conclude that the posters produced the change. It might have been something else, as suggested before. There might have been a change in the offerings at the tuckshop. There might have been a major television campaign at the same time. Other factors, not accounted for in this research, might have produced the result.

To use a longitudinal comparison research design you must:
1 Select variables that are related to the concepts under study.
2 Devise a way of measuring the variables.
3 Develop a data recording device.
4 Measure the same variables in the same way in two (or more) groups at two (or more) different times.

Such a research design is diagrammed in Figure 6.17. A research design like this can answer the question, 'Are Groups A and B different through time?' It cannot, however, explain why there was no difference, if that is the case, or prove what produced the difference, if there is a difference.

As with the comparison study, the longitudinal comparison study can be used as an approximation of the experimental design. The longitudinal comparison study may also make use of official statistics. From the data in Figure 6.16 the researcher

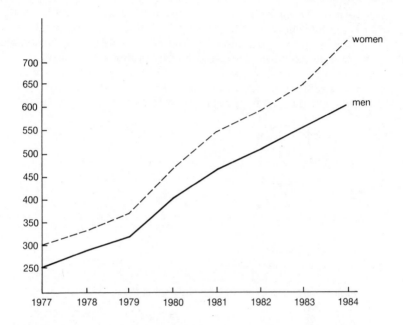

Figure 6.16 Index of average earnings: non-manual workers. UK. April 1970 = 100 *Employment Gazette*

can draw conclusions about the comparative earnings of men and women over time. The graph makes use of index numbers. These are often used in economic statistics to make comparisons easier. To construct an index number, a base year is chosen—in this case 1970. If the average earnings of men in that year were, say, £50 a week, that would be given a value of 100 and all subsequent earnings would be related to this. If earnings a year later had risen to £60, a rise of 20%, the index number would also be increased by 20%, to 120. If a few years later earnings had risen to £75, this would be a rise of 50% on the base year, so the index would also be increased by 50% to 150. Figure 6.16 shows that by 1977 the earnings of non-manual male workers had risen to about 250 compared to the base year of 1970 while the earnings of non-manual women workers had risen to just over 300. By 1984 men's pay on average was six times what it had been in 1970 while women's had grown nearly sevenfold. Note that while the Figure shows women's pay was rising faster, this does not mean that they were earning as much as men, because they started from a much lower level in 1970.

Similar data could be amassed to make other comparisons, using either index numbers or the original figures. For example, countries could be compared on birth-rates, death-rates, marriage rates, divorce rates, unemployment, inflation, and so on. The longitudinal comparison allows the researcher to compare the trends in data drawn from two different sources.

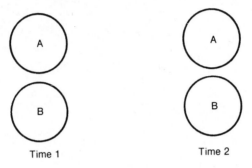

Figure 6.17 A diagram of a longitudinal comparison study

5   The experiment

If the aim of your research is to determine the effect that a change in one variable has upon another, an experimental design is required. While the other research designs provide useful information, the experimental design provides the most rigorous test of a hypothesis which specifies that X causes Y. The fundamental requirement of an experimental design is that the researcher has some control over variation in the independent variable and is able to control the influence of other variables.

The ideal form of the experimental design can be set out as follows. Let us take the hypothesis that a set of lessons on selecting nutritious snacks will promote healthier snack selection by students at the tuckshop. It can be diagrammed in this way:

In order to test this hypothesis using an experimental design the researcher must:

1 Select two groups of students. These two groups must be as alike as possible: same age, same proportion of boys to girls, taking same courses at school. They need to be the same, or as alike as possible, on any variable that might affect the dependent variable, or the relation between the independent variable and the dependent variable. A section on how to do this follows.
2 Devise measures for the variables. The dependent variable will be measured by a student snack selection checklist, completed by the students or by observation of the purchases at the shop. The independent variable is exposure to the lessons on nutritious snacks (yes or no).
3 Select one of the two classes of home economics students to be the control group. It will have lessons on something else while the experimental group has lessons on nutritious snacks.
4 The dependent variable will be measured before and after the lessons are given to both the control and the experimental group.
5 Because the groups are as alike as possible in all other respects and the only known difference between them is the exposure (or lack of it) to the lessons on nutritious snacks, any difference between the two groups' snack selection behaviour can be attributed to the lessons on nutritious snacks.

The diagram of the experimental design is shown in Figure 6.18. This research design asks the question, 'Is there a change in the difference between the experimental group and the control group following the manipulation of the

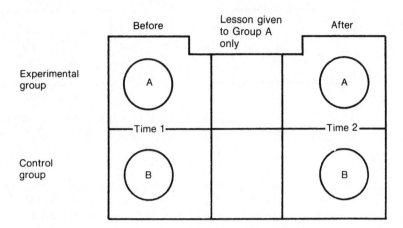

Figure 6.18 Diagram of experimental research design

Student snack selection at tuckshop 1 (in percentages)

	Before		After	
	A (Exp)	**B (Control)**	**A (Exp)**	**B (Control)**
Sweets	70	70	50	70
Fruit	20	20	40	20
Other	10	10	10	10

Figure 6.19 Hypothetical results of an experimental study

independent variable?' In this instance the manipulation of the independent variable is the giving of a lesson on nutritious snacks. Figures 6.19 and 6.20 provide two sets of hypothetical results. What would each set of results lead you to conclude?

What do you conclude from this table of data? Did the lesson have any impact on student snack selection?

What conclusion would you have to draw if the results were like those in Figure 6.20? Both groups changed, but they

Student snack selection at tuckshop 2 (in percentages)

	Before		After	
	A (Exp)	B (Control)	A (Exp)	B (Control)
Sweets	70	70	60	60
Fruit	20	20	30	30
Other	10	10	10	10

Figure 6.20 Hypothetical results of an experimental study

changed by the same amount. It would appear that the lesson had no effect. Make additional tables of possible results and interpret them. It is good practice. First make one in which the control group changes but the experimental group stays the same. What would you conclude?

How can an experimental research design test the hypothesis that amount of study is directly related to academic performance? Which is the independent variable? Which is the dependent variable? The operationalized form of this hypothesis we have been dealing with has been diagrammed as follows:

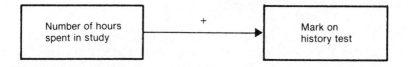

In order to design an experiment, the researcher must be able to manipulate, that is, to change the values of, the independent variable. How can the researcher exercise control over the independent variable in this hypothesis? How can hours of study be manipulated?

Here is an example. If the researcher had access to two similar history classes the following experiment could be conducted. Two passages of material could be assigned and students tested for their comprehension of the passages. In this instance comprehension is treated as one aspect of academic performance. The passages have been determined to be of similar difficulty. For the first test each student would have a total of 45 minutes to study the material. A month later the procedure is repeated using the second passage. But in the second trial, the experimental group was given a total of 75 minutes for study. The control group was allowed 45 minutes as they had been before. This research would be diagrammed:

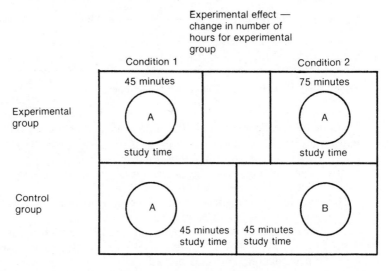

Figure 6.21 Diagram of experimental research design testing hypothesis on study time and academic performance

The independent variable, time spent in study, is manipulated by the researcher in such a way that the effect of change in the independent variable, if any, should be observable in change in the dependent variable, that is, scores on a comprehension test. Any change in the difference between the scores of the experimental group and the control group can be attributed to the change in the study time allowed each group, since the groups have been selected to be as alike as possible in all other respects. The results will be reported as average scores for each group since the researcher is interested in group performance rather than individual performance in this study.

Figures 6.22, 6.23 and 6.24 depict possible results of such an experiment. Let us assume that the possible scores on the comprehension test ranged from 0 to 100. How would you interpret the following results? Do the results in Figure 6.22 indicate that the amount of study time had any bearing on the results of two classes on the comprehension test? What about Figure 6.23?

Average results on comprehension tests for two
classes 1

	Condition 1	Condition 2
Experimental group	60%	80%
Control group	60%	60%

Figure 6.22 Hypothetical results of an experiment

Average results on comprehension tests for two
classes 2

	Condition 1	Condition 2
Experimental group	65%	70%
Control group	60%	65%

Figure 6.23 Hypothetical results of an experiment

Figure 6.23 presents a problem. The experimental group did
better than the control group under both conditions but both
groups improved from the first time to the second. It is *not*
possible to conclude that an increase in study time contributed
to the increase in results for the experimental group because the
control group increased by a similar amount.

Try Figure 6.24. What would you conclude from these
results? These results indicate that both groups improved but
that the experimental group showed substantially greater
improvement. A likely conclusion would be that some of the
improvement, that exhibited by both groups, was due to
increased skill in doing this sort of examination owing to the
practice both groups got writing the first test, but that the rest
of the improvement, that shown by the experimental group, was
due to the increase in study time. You may find it useful to put
other results in tables similar to those above and practise
interpreting hypothetical results.

Average results on comprehension tests for two classes 3

	Condition 1	Condition 2
Experimental group	65%	80%
Control group	60%	65%

Figure 6.24 Hypothetical results of an experiment

In summary, an experimental research design is used to determine whether changes in the independent variable actually produce changes in the dependent variable. Does a change in X cause a change in Y? If you are planning to design an experiment consult the following checklist.

Checklist for designing an experiment

1 Are you able to manipulate the independent variable? Are you able to introduce it, or give it to the experimental group, like the lessons on nutritious snack selection? Or are you able to change it for the experimental group, like the number of hours two classes have to prepare for an exam? Many independent variables are not able to be manipulated satisfactorily. This may be due to our sense of what is ethical (right or wrong). For example, we do not arbitrarily move babies from one carer to another in order to assess the impact of the change.

2 Are you able to select two groups (or more) that are alike in all essential ways, one of which will become the control group and the other the *experimental group* (the group that gets the treatment)? Are you able to isolate the two groups so that the experimental group does not communicate with or otherwise affect the control group?

3 Are you able to measure the dependent variable for each group both before and after the change in the independent variable? An experiment requires before and after measures of the dependent variable for both the experimental and the control group.

4 Have you recorded your data and presented your findings in such a way that you can draw conclusions about the effect (or lack of it) on the dependent variable?

If you can answer yes to these questions then you have designed an experimental study to test your hypothesis. You must be able to answer yes to the first two questions in order to eliminate other possible explanations for the relationship between X and Y. By carefully controlling for other variables by studying two groups as alike as possible and by manipulating the independent variable you come as close as possible to proving that X causes Y.

How do you choose a research design?

Now that each type of research design has been described, you may be wondering how you choose between them. It is important to remember that each design provides the answer to a particular kind of question. Hence one of the first considerations in selecting a research design is, 'What kind of question is being asked?' Following is a summary table of research designs and the questions each asks. Review it to refresh your memory of each design.

Type of design			Question asked
1 Simple case study			
Ⓐ			What is happening?
2 Longitudinal study			
Ⓐ	Ⓐ		Has there been a change
Time 1	Time 2		in A?
3 Comparison			
Ⓐ			
			Are A and B different?
Ⓑ			
4 Longitudinal comparison			
Ⓐ	Ⓐ		Are A and B different through
Ⓑ	Ⓑ		time?
Time 1	Time 2		
5 Experiment			
Experimental group	Ⓐ	↓ Ⓐ	Is the difference between A and B due to a change (↓ in
Control group	Ⓑ	Ⓑ	the independent variable?
	Time 1	Time 2	

Figure 6.25 The five basic types of research design

If the hypothesis you are testing asks, 'Does a change in the independent variable produce a change in the dependent variable?', then an experimental design is required. This sounds harsh, but it is true. However, an experiment is not always possible. What can be done then? Use one of the other research designs, realising that it is not ideal. Make sure that you draw only such conclusions as your data and research design permit. Note the fact that your research is limited because of your use of a research design other than an experimental design. The limitations section of your report is the place to demonstrate that you know what the ideal is and that you know your work is not completely ideal.

Controlling for the influence of other variables

At a number of points in this chapter we have referred to the possibility that other variables, not included in the study, might have been responsible for observed variation in the dependent variable. This is one of the greatest fears of a researcher—the results may be due to something else. For example it might have been that the change in snack selection was due to a change in the price of lollies (up) and apples (down), and not to the lessons on nutritious snacks. Or the improvement in students' performance in an exam might be due to increased skill in taking such exams and not to the increase in study time. For such reasons as these it is important to control for the influence of all other variables which might have some bearing on the variables under study.

How does the researcher control for the influence of other variables? There are several key points here. The most important one is to be aware of the fact that other variables may come into play. As you design a piece of research it is important to keep a list of other potentially influential variables. You may or may not eventually do anything about them, but it is important to be aware of such variables. All scientific conclusions are drawn tentatively, in part because of the impossibility of controlling for everything. Thus the first step is to be aware of the possible influence of other variables.

The second step is to take some of these variables into account when you design your study. Should all the people studied be of the same sex, roughly the same age, attend the same school, be in the same class, be from the same suburb? The way you draw your sample (see Chapter 8) may be influenced by your concern about control variables. If two groups being compared are supposed to be similar except for one variable, then the researcher must ensure that they are, or acknowledge this limitation of the research.

For example, recall the comparison study of infant growth and development. If you had reason to believe that there might be a difference in the growth patterns of boy babies as compared with girl babies, you might choose to limit your study to girl babies. If you felt that growth patterns might be affected by stages in the life cycle, you might ensure that all the infants studied were studied for the same period of their life (e.g. from one week after birth for eight weeks). If you felt that the mothers' nutritional status might affect the growth rate of babies being breast-fed, you might decide to ensure that all the nursing mothers had similar diets. These are some ways of controlling or limiting the influence of variables not a part of the study. In general, the more variables you can eliminate by making the groups under study similar, the better.

The most important point about controls is to be aware of the possible influence of other variables, to select groups in such a way as to eliminate the influence of as many such variables as possible and to note the others in the limitations section of your report.

Questions for review

1 What basic question is answered by research design?
2 List the five types of research design. Diagram each design. What question does each ask?
3 Why is the case study said to be the basic building block of all research design?
4 What is required to do a longitudinal study?
5 What is required to do a comparison study?
6 What is required to do a longitudinal comparison study?
7 What are the key features of an experiment?
8 On what bases does a researcher choose a research design?
9 Why is it important to control for other variables?
10 How does one control for other variables?
11 What is done about variables over which the researcher has no control?

7

Selecting a sample

How to select a sample
Types of sampling procedure
Determining sample size
Summary
Questions for review

To whom are you going to administer your questionnaire?
Which history class will be the subject of your experiments?
Which babies will be weighed and measured? Since it is
impossible to weigh all babies, administer questionnaires to
everyone, and experiment on all history classes, researchers
select samples for research. Indeed, it is often more desirable to
study a sample than to try to study the whole population. A
carefully drawn sample not only makes the task possible, it
often produces more accurate results.

We use sampling and we generalize from the samples we draw
in our everyday life. If we want to check the weather we look
out of the window and judge the weather as a whole from the
sample that we can see through the window. Other forms of
sampling and generalization follow the same logic. Care is taken
to make sure the sample is an accurate reflection of the whole
from which it is taken. In the case of the weather, we may look
out of windows on different sides of the house before drawing a
conclusion (i.e. generalizing our findings from our sample).
Sampling is an important feature of all research. Part of the
whole is studied and the results are taken to be an accurate
reflection of the whole.

The most important point to remember about sampling is:

The manner in which the sample is drawn determines to what
extent we can generalize from the findings.

Only if the sample studied can be shown to represent a larger population can the results of a study of the sample be taken to give reliable information about the larger population. If the sample studied is not representative, the conclusions drawn from the research must be limited to the sample studied.

For example, you might have developed a short questionnaire on attitudes toward nuclear weapons. If you had twenty of your friends, schoolmates, and relatives fill out your questionnaire, the results would be limited to that group of twenty people. On the other hand, if you had selected a sample of twenty people which accurately reflected the views of a larger group of two hundred (for example, all the sixth-formers in a particular school) you could draw conclusions about the two hundred from the results of a study of the sample of twenty. In the first instance your findings were limited to the twenty people studied. In the second you could generalize the results to the larger population which your sample represented.

While sampling the weather is relatively easy, sampling groups of people is rather more complicated. The basic problem is to select a sample that accurately reflects a specified larger group. Several techniques for drawing samples from groups of people have been devised by social scientists. The most basic and potentially useful of these techniques will be described in this chapter. The strengths and weaknesses of each will be discussed in order to help you select a technique appropriate to your research.

It should also be remembered that for some purposes sampling is not required. If the researcher is not interested in drawing conclusions for a larger population than that actually studied, sampling is not needed. For example, a psychologist might decide to study her baby's cognitive development. Only one baby, hers, is needed for the study. Why would she not be able to draw conclusions about all babies, or even other babies in her family? It is usually dangerous to rely on the observation of a single case to provide an accurate picture of a large group. It would be like an American forming an opinion of all British people after meeting just one. Depending upon which British person was the basis of this 'case study', the most amazing and misleading impressions would be formed. In studies of single cases, generalizations cannot be safely drawn. There is no way of knowing whether the case studied will give an accurate impression of the whole.

The second situation in which sampling is not an issue occurs when the researcher is interested only in one small group which is easily studied as a whole. If the interest is in the performance of one history class, or the comparison of two groups of students, for example those who did, compared with those who did not have lessons on nutritious snack selection, then sampling is not an issue. In these instances the whole population is being studied. So long as the researcher is willing to limit the conclusions drawn to those actually studied, sampling is not a problem. If, however, the researcher wants to generalize, that is to draw conclusions about a large group on the basis of the study of a few, then a sampling procedure must be selected.

Why do researchers sample? Samples are used to reduce the cost in time, energy, and money of studying large populations. It is often simply not possible or desirable to study everyone. Samples of large groups are drawn in order to gain a reliable picture of the larger group by studying a carefully selected smaller number of that population. The way in which the sample is selected determines whether or not reliable conclusions about the larger group can be drawn on the basis of the study of smaller numbers.

How to select a sample

What do you want to know? About whom do you want to know it? These are the questions to answer first. Given that it is impossible to know everything about everyone or all groups, selections must be made. First decide *what* you want to know. You did this when you formed a hypothesis, focused it, and made it operational. You devised instruments and designed research. Once these things are done, attention is turned to the second question, *about whom* do you want to know what it is you want to know?

The first step in sample selection is to identify the population about which you want to know something. Think back to your hypothesis. For example, the hypothesis about amount of study and academic performance relates to students. The largest possible population would be all students in the world at any time past, present, and future. That would be an impossible population to sample. You may decide to limit your sample to students in English universities. That is still a very large and diverse population. You might decide to limit your focus to the children in a particular school. Finally, you might decide that making generalizations about all students everywhere is not so important and you are happy to settle for finding out what is happening in two classes in a school.

Remember! It is perfectly legitimate to select any population as the object of your study.

The population about which you wish to generalize will affect your selection of a sampling procedure. Once you have decided about whom you want to be able to draw reliable conclusions, you are ready to select a sampling procedure. What other practical factors might help you to decide which population you wish to be able to generalize to? Think about time and money.

Types of sampling procedure

There are basically two types of sampling procedure: random and non-random. A random sampling procedure provides the greatest assurance that those selected are a representative sample of the larger group. If a non-random sampling procedure is used, one can only hope that those selected for study bear some likeness to the larger group.

Non-random sampling procedures

Non-random sampling procedures include accidental sampling, accidental quota sampling, purposive sampling, and systematic matching sampling. While useful for many studies, non-random sampling procedures provide only a weak basis for generalization.

Accidental sampling

This sampling procedure involves using what is immediately available. A teacher studies his own class. A psychologist studies her own children. A nutritionist studies the impact of diet change on his children. A student studies the interaction patterns of the families of two friends and a cousin. These are all accidental samples. The persons, families, and classes studied were selected because they were available, not because they were known to be representative of some larger group.

Some people confuse accidental sampling with random sampling. Persons met at random, that is accidentally, do not comprise a random sample. The problem with accidental samples is that the researcher does not know in what ways the sample is biased. How is the sample a misleading representative of the larger population of which information is desired? There is no way of checking this without doing a study of everyone, or a study of a properly drawn random sample.

The people on a given street at a given time will be a biased sample of residents of that suburb. Such an accidental sample will not give you reliable information about the residents of the suburb. A questionnaire on attitudes towards abortion given to every tenth person encountered at a suburban shopping centre will not provide a reliable indication of the opinions of residents of the suburb. It will only tell you the opinions of people who shop at that place at that hour on that day of the week. If you are interested in the opinions of the residents of the suburb, an accidental sample of Tuesday morning shoppers will not provide the information.

Similarly, the families you know will be a biased sample of families in your city. They may be members of the same clubs, churches, political parties, or at similar stages in the family life cycle. In the same way students in a particular class or school will be a biased sample of students. Think of ways in which the students in your class would be a biased sample of students in your school. This is why *the results of a study of an accidental sample apply only to the sample studied*.

An accidental sampling procedure is appropriate if you do not intend to draw conclusions about a larger group on the basis of the group you study. Accidental samples are handy, require little effort, and are useful for many studies. The major disadvantage is that the findings of a study of an accidental sample are strictly limited to those studied.

Accidental quota sampling

In an accidental sampling procedure the researcher does not know in what ways the sample is biased because it is uncertain which aspects of the total population are included and which are not. This difficulty can be partially overcome through a quota sampling procedure. In an accidental quota sampling procedure the researcher selects individuals or groups *on the basis of set criteria*. A researcher comparing the opinions of males and females might set a quota of 50 males and 50 females. This will ensure that the sample studied has both females and males present in it. Another researcher comparing the performance of history classes and English classes might specify that the sample must contain four of each type of class. Someone interested in the difference between students from different schools, or social classes, or incomes, or ethnic groups, might specify in advance the number or proportion of each desired in the sample.

Perhaps a more developed example will help. Presume you are interested in comparing the attitudes held by secondary school students from different ethnic groups towards university. In order to make sure that the sample you study has in it students from each of the ethnic groups, you might set a quota of 10 students from each of the ethnic groups you wished to compare. By selecting 10 students from each ethnic group, that is by filling your quota, you make sure that your sample includes people or groups with certain specified characteristics (in this instance, ethnic background).

Quota sampling is useful when a particular group or characteristic is relatively rare in the population. By setting a quota, and selecting people until the quota is filled, the group or characteristics you want in the sample are there.

Quota sampling, however, suffers most of the same defects as accidental sampling. Can you see why? Although the researcher is assured of the presence of certain categories in the sample, for example, males and females or people from West Indian, Pakistani, Indian, or Chinese backgrounds, the representativeness of the sample is still not ensured. This is due to the fact that the individuals, or groups, are not selected randomly. The sample may have 50 males and 50 females but of whom are these males and females representative? This is not known. The sample selected may have 10 students from each ethnic background. But it is not know whether the West Indian students are an unbiased sample of West Indian students. It is not known whether a study of the 10 students with an Indian background will provide reliable information about other students with this background. In other words, it is risky to draw conclusions about a larger group from an accidental quota sample of that group. None the less, this sampling procedure is often used due to the pressures of time and budget. Conclusions drawn are strictly limited to those actually studied. Tentative implications for others may be suggested.

Purposive sampling

Some researchers believe that they can, using their own judgement or intuition, select the best people or groups to be studied. The *typical* rural school is selected and studied, and the results generalized to rural schools. The *typical* English class is compared with the *typical* history class. How are these known to be typical? Unless objective criteria are set out beforehand, and each group shown to meet these criteria, there is no way of knowing. However, there are times when this is the only practical way to draw a sample. If a purposive sample is studied only tentatively suggested generalizations may be made. The conclusions drawn from a comparison of a few *typical* rural schools with a few *typical* urban schools might be phrased in this way: 'The results of this study comparing three rural and three urban schools have revealed the following six major differences. While it is not strictly possible to generalize from this sample to all rural and urban schools we think it is likely that these differences will be found in other instances.' Carefully qualify any tentative conclusions you might wish to draw on the basis of a study of a purposive sample.

Systematic matching sampling

There are times, especially when a researcher wants to compare two groups of very different sizes, when a systematic matching sampling procedure may be used. A study comparing female and male headteachers of secondary schools in an area in terms of career satisfaction would be an example. There are so few female secondary heads at present that the researcher would most likely study the entire population in the area. However, for the comparison, the researcher might select a matched sample of male heads. Let us say 10 female heads had been identified for study. Rather than examining all male heads, or a random sample, 10 male heads would be selected. Each of the 10 male heads would have been selected because they matched a female head in certain features deemed to be important to the consideration of career satisfaction. Examples of such matching features might be: age, length of service in position, education, marital status, size and type of school served, and career ambition. Even though the claim to representativeness is weak, this sampling procedure is often a suitable compromise when comparing groups of extremely different size.

These examples of non-random sampling procedures are given because they are frequently used by researchers. If a non-random sampling procedure is used the researcher must be aware of the limitations to the conclusions drawn. Technically, the conclusions drawn from a study of a non-random sample are limited to that sample and cannot be used for further generalizations. Read through some research literature in your library. Can you find an example of non-random sampling being used?

Random sampling procedures

Random sampling procedures provide the greatest assurance that the sample drawn accurately represents the population. There are three basic random sampling procedures: simple random sampling, stratified random sampling, and cluster sampling.

Simple random sampling

This is the ideal method of drawing a sample. It is, however, very difficult to do. A simple random sampling procedure guarantees that each element (person, group, class, school, etc.) in the population has an equal chance of being selected *and* that every possible combination of the specified number of elements has an equal chance of selection. The mathematics of such selection procedures is very complex and beyond the scope of this text. Those interested might consider the appropriate parts of the following sources on sampling procedure:

Ackroyd, S., and Hughes, J. A., (1981) *Data Collection in Context*, Longman, London

Hoinville, G., Jowell, R., and associates, (1978) *Survey Research Practice*, Heinemann, London

Sudman, S., (1976) *Applied Sampling*, Academic Press, New York and London

Ferman, G. S., and Levin, J., (1975) *Social Science Research: A Handbook for Students*, Schenkman, New York

Moser, C., and Kalton, G., (1971, reprinted 1985) *Survey Methods in Social Investigation*, Gower, Aldershot.

In order to draw a simple random sample the researcher must:

1 Identify the population from which the sample is to be drawn.
2 Enumerate and list each element (or persons, households, car owners, etc.) in the population.
3 Devise a method of selection which ensures that each element has the same probability of selection and that each combination of the total number of elements has the same probability of selection.

Given the virtual impossibility of meeting all these criteria, it is not surprising that a number of acceptable compromises have been devised. Essentially the task is to devise some form of a fair lottery in which each combination of numbers has an equal chance of coming up.

The first set of compromise random sampling procedures involves studies in which it is possible to identify and enumerate the total population. For example, while possible, it would be too much work for most purposes to try to identify and enumerate the total population of people taking A levels in a particular year. It would be possible to identify and enumerate those students taking A levels in a particular school. Other relatively easy to enumerate populations include: all the members of a particular club, the students in a history class, the teachers in a school, all the children in a particular nursery school, or people in a home for the elderly, or people whose name is in a telephone directory, on a voters' list, or all the maintained secondary schools in a particular area. The telephone directory may pose particular problems. If the city is large, do you enumerate all the subscribers? What about non-representativeness—since it only includes subscribers and usually only one name for each household? In what ways would a voter registration roll be biased? Once identified and enumerated (that is, numbered from beginning to end) a sample may be selected.

Here is an example. You want to study a simple random sample of the 250 first-year students in a particular school. The first step is done. You have identified the population. The second step is to identify and enumerate each element in the population. In this instance the elements are the 250 students. The students will have to be listed and numbered from 1 to 250.

   1 Jane Allsmith
   2 Janette Attwood
   3 George Black
   4 Henry Buck
     . . .
 250 Mildred Zylska

Once this is done the whole population to which you want to generalize the findings of your study is identified and enumerated. It is now possible to move to the next step, selecting the sample. We will deal with issues of sample size later in the chapter. Let us assume that you decided to draw a sample of 50 students from the larger population of 250 students.

The most acceptable form of selecting a sample from an enumerated population involves the use of a table of random numbers. Such a table appears as an appendix to this book. A starting point in the table is picked (usually by the accidental fall of the point of a pen) and those elements of the population whose numbers come up in the table of random numbers as you move down the column from the starting-point are selected until your sample size is achieved. In order to draw the sample of 50 students from 250 first-formers by this procedure you would do the following. Remember each student has been given a number from 1 to 250. Figure 7.1 is a section from a table of random numbers. Because the numbers you need to select have between one and three digits (or are comprised of three digits 001 to 250), you will use the first three digits. The next step is to select a starting-point. This can be done by closing your eyes and pointing a pen at the table and starting there. It is permissible to move up or down the columns as the numbers are random. That is, there is no pattern in the table. The numbers are in no particular order. Let us say your pen landed on number 161.

28071	03528	89714
48210	48761	▷02365
83417	20219	82900
20531	43657	45100
94654	97801	01153
52839	42986	28100
74591	▷16100	91478
38921	56913	32675
40759	84027	52831
45980	70523	47985
52182	68194	62783
12890	59208	00691
08523	74312	13542

Figure 7.1 Using a table of random numbers

The first element (or student) selected is number 161. If you decided to move down the columns the next number to be selected would be the next number in the range 001 to 250 that was not 161 (since 161 has already been selected). In this table it would be element (student) numbered 023. The next would be student 011, then 006, then 135. And you would go on to the next column. You would continue this procedure until you had selected a total of 50 students. You would then have a simple random sample of 50 students which could be taken to be reliably representative of the 250.

To give yourself practice, start again at number 161, but move up the columns. Which numbers would then be selected?

A different sample of 50 would of course be drawn, but because it was randomly selected the results of a study of it will also give reliable information about the whole group. Indeed, one would expect only the smallest difference between a study of the first sample and a study of the second.

Another acceptable form of selection is to put all the names or numbers in a hat and draw out the number required. To ensure that each element and combination of elements has the same probability of selection, each time a selection is made the name or number should be returned to the hat. But this is a technicality. In the event that a number is drawn more than once, it is simply returned to the hat, but the number is not selected twice.

The random selection of a sample of 50 students from 250 according to this method would require that all the names of the students, or a set of numbers from 001 to 250 be put in a container. The container would be shaken before each draw. The first 50 students whose names (or numbers) are drawn form the sample.

While these techniques are somewhat laborious and time consuming they do provide the most reliable sample procedures. The simple random sample is the ideal.

Systemic sampling

A systematic sampling procedure involves the selection of every n^{th} case in a list. Again the population must be identified, but it is not necessary to enumerate the list. For example if you had a list of 400 students in a school and you wanted a sample of 80, you might select every fifth name on the list. To draw a systematic sample you need to know the total number in the group and the number you want in the sample. By dividing the total number by the sample number you find the interval at which you will select.

```
Total population = 400
Sample desired   = 80
Interval         = 400 ÷ 80 = 5
```

In the event of an uneven number for the interval, the nearest whole number is selected for the interval.

```
Total population = 393
Sample desired   = 80
Interval         = 393 ÷ 80 = 4.9 → 5
```

The critical step in systematic sampling is to select the first case randomly. To do this one of the first elements (names, groups, numbers, or schools) in the long list must be selected. If the interval is 5, one of the first 5 must be selected as the starting-point. If the interval is 10, then one of the first 10 must be selected, and so on. The easiest way to make a random selection is to put all the numbers (1 to 5, or to 10, or whatever) in a container, shake it, and draw out a number. That number will be your starting-point. Or you could close your eyes and pick out one of the elements in the first interval. The first element must be selected randomly. Once the first element (in the case of our list of names of students, the first name) is selected, then each nth element (whatever the interval) thereafter is selected. In the example of the list of students at a school, the list had 400 names and the interval was 5. Let us presume that the number 4 was the number that was drawn out of the container. Then the selection would start with the fourth student on the list. Count four more and the next one is selected. Count four more and the next is selected.

S. Aaron	D. Enticott
J. Adams	R. Farah
K. Adams	I. Grozdanovski
*M. Belanti	*S. Harris
A. Bordignon	. . .
P. Bourne	M. Todorovic
N. Bradley	E. Warnecke
L. Brookman	B. Wignell
*E. Chatterly	G. Yates
H. Donaldson	

If one of the names selected is unavailable, or has dropped out of school, a replacement is selected in the first instance by drawing the name just before, and in the second instance by drawing the name just after. If M. Belanti had dropped out, K. Adams would be the replacement. If E. Chatterly had also dropped out H. Donaldson would be the replacement. Another replacement strategy is to flip a coin (heads: name before, tails: name after). Note, names are replaced only if they are genuinely unavailable, not because the researcher might prefer someone else to be in the sample.

A systematic sampling procedure provides an acceptable approximation of the ideals of the simple random sampling procedure. It certainly helps to overcome researcher bias in sample selection. The selection goes on independently of the researcher's preferences or inclinations or prejudices. So long as any biases in the ordering of the list do not occur at the same interval as the sampling interval, a reasonably reliable sample will be drawn by this procedure.

Stratified random sampling

This sampling procedure is similar to quota sampling, outlined above, except that each sub-section or stratum of the population to be studied is identified and enumerated and elements drawn from it by a random sampling procedure. You may wish to compare types of schools in terms of the overall performance of students. Let us say that you have an overall performance measure for each secondary school in a particular local authority. A simple random sample of schools might not provide enough cases in some of the categories of analysis you intended to use. You might classify the schools into urban, suburban, and rural schools. Having done that, the schools in each group would be identified and enumerated and a random sample of each group identified.

For example you might want to compare the attitudes toward nuclear disarmament held by students studying maths and science with those studying humanities. Rather than do a simple random sample of the students in a school, you would identify all students in each category, list them separately, and draw a sample from each list using one of the random selection processes outlined above (using a table of random numbers or drawing names from a hat or systematic sampling).

There are a variety of criteria used to stratify populations (that is to divide a large group into smaller more finely defined groups). Some examples are: age (you might want to compare people of different ages); stage in the life cycle; gender; occupation; ethnicity; location (rural vs. urban); size (large school vs. small school). The criterion for stratification will be suggested by your hypothesis. A hypothesis comparing males with females may be best studied using a stratified random sample—one in which a random sample of males is compared with a random sample of females. A hypothesis comparing high income families with low income families, or early school leavers with university graduates, or teachers with students, might lead the researcher to use a stratified random sampling procedure.

Cluster sampling

The fact that simple random sampling becomes tremendously complex and costly for large and scattered populations has led to the development of cluster sampling procedures. Cluster sampling procedures usually involve several *stages* of random selections. Rather than enumerating the whole population, the population is divided into segments. Then several of the segments are chosen at random. Elements within each segment are then selected randomly following identification and enumeration. In this way only the elements in the selected segment need to be identified and enumerated.

National samples are usually drawn on a multi-stage cluster sample procedure. So are samples of cities. For example a sample of households in Birmingham might be drawn by dividing Birmingham into the wards used in council elections. A number of wards could be drawn at random. Within each ward, election districts (i.e. the places where people vote) would be identified and enumerated and a random sample of election districts drawn. Finally, the residences in each election district would be identified and enumerated and a random sample of residences selected on the basis of an unbiased rule of selection. In this way a random sample of the residences of Birmingham would be approximated. Cluster sampling procedures have been devised to provide a reliably random, hence representative, sample of a large population without having to identify and enumerate the entire population at the outset. In this procedure only smaller randomly selected segments (clusters) have to be identified and enumerated.

The essentials of the basic forms of sampling have been presented. How do you select a procedure for your research? This depends largely on the population about which you wish to draw conclusions. If you are happy to limit your conclusion to the students in your class, that accidental sample will do perfectly well. If the demands of time and expense force you to examine a sub-group of larger population, one of the random sampling procedures should be used. The extra effort pays great dividends in the value of the research conclusions. For a relatively small amount of effort you can dramatically increase the representativeness of the findings and reduce the influence of any bias on the part of the researcher.

Random sampling procedures are particularly important in research which aims to assess the attitudes, values, or beliefs of a population. Public opinion polls usually use a form of random sampling. On the basis of their samples such pollsters predict how people will vote, what brands of detergent they will buy, and in what direction popular tastes are shifting.

Finally, it is impossible to generalize from most case studies, because a single element drawn from a larger population, be it a family, a baby, a class, a school, or a country, is too small a sample, even if drawn randomly, to be representative of the population. We will deal with the problem of sample size in the next section of this chapter.

Determining sample size

How large a sample do you need? This is a very difficult question to answer. If the population you wish to sample is fairly homogeneous, that is, the relevant characteristics are fairly evenly distributed, a smaller sample can be relied on than if the population is highly variable. Several basic issues need to be considered in determining sample size.

First, if statistics are going to be used in the analysis and interpretation of data there are usually requirements for sample size. We will not elaborate on these requirements since this text takes a non-statistical approach to the research process. Professional researchers must take these considerations into account.

Secondly, the more accurately the data must reflect the total population, the larger will be the sample. In research done for market analysis and for social science surveys, very large numbers are selected.

Thirdly, the more questions asked, the more controls introduced, the greater the detail of the analysis of the data, the larger the sample will have to be in order to provide sufficient data for the analysis. In professional research, samples of hundreds and thousands will be drawn to accommodate this demand.

It is important to remember that large samples are more convincing to those who hear about the study than small samples. Large samples simply have more clout. You may produce startling findings and novel results, but if your sample is too small you will probably be ignored.

While all the above factors seem to argue for larger and larger samples, considerations of cost—time, money, and effort—argue for the limitation of sample size.

Most of the research you will read about in journals or papers is based on large samples, but we have a few suggestions regarding sample size for student projects. Since the importance of these projects is to learn basic research skills rather than to produce results that are generalized to large populations, several basic compromises are possible. Our suggestions for student projects take the form of two basic rules.

The first basic rule about sample size states that about thirty individuals are required in order to provide a pool large enough for even the simple kinds of analyses.

The second basic rule is that you need a sample large enough to ensure that it is theoretically possible for each cell in your analytical table to have five cases fall in it. A few examples will make this clear. Remember the study of snack selection. Student snack selections were categorized according to the table in Figure 7.2.

Sweet	Fruit	Other

Figure 7.2 A dummy table for the categorization of student snack selection

Figure 7.2 is usually referred to as a dummy table. It is a table prepared before the collection of data to help to focus the issues of the research, to guide data collection, and to help determine sample size. In this case the data recording form, dummy table, and final table for presentation of data take the same form. This dummy table has 3 cells. The minimum sample size for this study would be $3 \times 5 = 15$; but it would still be preferable to have 30 because of the first basic rule regarding minimum sample size.

One of the comparative studies suggested before in the study of student snack selection involved home economics students and non home economics students. The dummy table for such a study looked like Figure 7.3. This dummy table has 6 cells, hence the sample size required would be $6 \times 5 = 30$. Moreover, this study involves comparing two groups of students. Since each group is accorded 3 cells in the table each group requires a sample of $3 \times 5 = 15$. You might select either a quota, or stratified random, or cluster sampling

Snack selected	Home economics students	Non home economics students
Sweet		
Fruit		
Other		

Figure 7.3 A dummy table comparing snack selections of home economics and non home economics students

procedure to draw a sample of at least 15 of each group of students.

It is at this stage that the impact of adding variables to the analysis can be made most clearly. It is always a temptation to add a variable. Indeed you may have good reason to want to try to assess the impact of a variety of variables. Moreover, professional research often analyses many variables. However, the addition of one variable will increase the sample size required and the complexity of analysing the data. Again the use of dummy tables is very helpful in clarifying this for the researcher. By adding one variable to the analysis of student snack selection the sample size was doubled and the size of the dummy table doubled. If we were to add another variable, let us say gender, we would require two tables like that in Figure 7.3, one for males and one for females. The sample size would be $12 \times 5 = 60$. A single dummy table for such a study would look like Figure 7.4.

Snack selection	Males		Females	
	Home economics students	Non home economics students	Home economics students	Non Home economics students
Sweet				
Fruit				
Other				

Figure 7.4 A dummy table for a study of student snack selection comparing males with females and home economics with non home economics students

To add yet another variable, let us say, year in school (first form, second form) would require yet another doubling of sample size and add further complexity to data analysis.

What would the dummy table look like for a study of the impact of amount of time studied on mark received in a history exam? In our previous use of this example we used a line graph to present possible results. A second use of dummy tables can now be seen. They help us to specify categories of analysis and data collection. The data collection sheet suggested for this study (Chapter 5, p. 82, Figure 5.4) asked the student to keep track of the amount of time spent in revision and the mark received in a history examination. For each student the data summarization form (Chapter 5, p. 83) recorded total time and mark. The number of students required for your sample depends on how you are going to analyse your data. A minimum of about thirty is required regardless of the form of analysis. But if you were planning to use tabular analysis the number of cells in the table would also play a role in determining sample size.

It would be possible to have a very large table with a column for every possible mark from 0 to 100. That would require a sample of 500 if only one category of time spent studying were used (two thousand if two categories of amount of time spent studying were used, etc.). Needless to say, that is not suitable for our purposes. Hence a smaller number of categories for reporting and analysing both the dependent variable (marks) and the independent variable (time spent in studying) must be found. The simplest categorization for marks would be pass/fail. But that might not be satisfactory. You might prefer fail, 50–64, 65–74, 75 +. That would be four categories of marks (see Figures 7.5 and 7.6).

Then there is the problem of finding categories for the amount of time spent in revision. This poses a different kind of problem. Again you could have a row in your table for each possible value reported from 0 to perhaps 120 hours. This suffers from the same fault as does having a column for each possible mark. Taken together such a table would require $100 \times 120 \times 5 = 60,000$ students in the sample. How are number of hours to be categorized? You will not know until the data are collected what the range of values are. But you might decide to have two categories, high and low. When the data have been gathered you determine what the average (or mean) number of hours studied is. All those above average are categorized high and those below are categorized low. Or you might decide to have three categories: high, moderate, and low. In this case you divide the sample into three even groups, those with the highest number of hours, a moderate number, and the lowest number. It is best to work this out first because of the implications for your sample size. Figures 7.5 and 7.6 demonstrate this.

Number of hours spent in revision	Examination result	
	Pass	**Fail**
High		
Low		

Figure 7.5 A dummy table for a study of the impact of number of hours spent in revision on examination results using two categories for each variable

In Figure 7.5 two categories are used for the analysis of each variable. The sample required for such a study could be $4 \times 5 = 20$ (30 would be better). In Figure 7.6 four categories are used for the dependent variable and three for the independent variable. The sample size required is $4 \times 3 \times 5 = 60$.

Hours spent in revision	Examination result			
	Fail	**50–64**	**65–74**	**75 +**
High				
Average				
Low				

Figure 7.6 A dummy table for a study of the impact of number of hours spent in revision on examination results using four categories for the dependent variable and three for the independent variable

The role of dummy tables can now be seen. They focus the research. They help to determine the categories of analysis of the data. They help to determine sample size. By devising dummy tables *before* collecting data the researcher is prevented from collecting more data than are actually going to be used.

There is no point in collecting data which will not go into the tables. What is to become of them? The researcher is also guided in sample selection by decisions about data analysis. In this way neither too much nor too little data are collected for the purpose of analysis.

A few more examples may help to clarify this important procedure. What samples are required for longitudinal or comparative studies? Take the example of a before and after longitudinal study. In such a study the same group is studied at two points in time. Hence the determination of sample size is made by one of the tables (either before or after), since they are presumably the same. Were they different, comparison would be made unnecessarily difficult. Refer back to the example of a longitudinal study in Chapter 6. Because the same group is measured twice, there needs to be a sufficient sample of that group in each measurement. The before and after measures each have three categories, hence the minimum sample would be $3 \times 5 = 15$.

Let us turn to the example of the questionnaire developed to assess attitudes towards the use of nuclear materials (Chapter 5, p. 92). Data produced by questionnaires have to be categorized just like test results or number of hours spent in revision. Like test results, scales on a questionnaire have a theoretical range. For the questionnaire on nuclear materials the range was from a low of 5 (indicating agreement with anti-nuclear statements) to a high of 20 (indicating disagreement with such statements). It is unlikely that you would want a table with 15 columns for this dependent variable. It will have to be categorized. High versus low agreement, or high, medium, and low agreement, are two possibilities. If you were comparing two groups, let us say a sample from the Church of England with a sample from the Methodists, your dummy table might look like that in Figure 7.7.

Position on use of nuclear material	Church of England	Methodists
Agreement		
Disagreement		

Figure 7.7 A dummy table for a study comparing the views of two groups on the use of nuclear material

The sample for this study would comprise a minimum of ten from each group. This might be achieved by a quota or a stratified random or a cluster sampling procedure. Which would be best and why? The example of a study of sexist attitudes among secondary school boys provides another opportunity to examine the utility of dummy tables. The questionnaire suggested for such a study is found in Chapter 5, p. 86. The hypothesis was:

> Boys who have gone to single-sex schools are more sexist in their attitudes towards women than boys who have attended co-educational schools.

The independent variable is type of school attended, single-sex v. co-educational. The dependent variable is sexist attitudes as measured by responses to a five-item scale. The independent variable has two categories: single-sex v. co-educational schooling (three if you include the 'mixed' category). Hence the table for analysing the data will have two columns, one for each category (again, three if the 'mixed' category is included).

How is the dependent variable to be categorized? Again it is unlikely that one row would be used for each of the twenty possible scores on the sexism scale. This would require a table with twenty rows. One alternative is to reduce the number of categories used to present and analyse the dependent variable. An example follows. The way the scale was constructed, agreement indicated a sexist orientation and disagreement a lack of sexism. The mid-point on this scale was fifteen. A score below fifteen could be taken to indicate low sexism. A score of fifteen and above could be taken to indicate high sexism. This would give two categories for the dependent variable. The break-point in

Sexism score	Educational context	
	Single sex school	Co-educational school
High		
Low		

Figure 7.8 A dummy table for a study of the impact of educational context on sexist attitudes among secondary school boys

the categories in this instance is determined by the nature of the scale. Since there are two categories for the dependent variable the table for analysing data will have two rows.

Figure 7.8 presents a dummy table for this study. The minimum sample for this study would be twenty, ten boys from each educational context. If the researcher decided to use three categories for the sexism score, the minimum sample would be thirty. If the researcher decided to include a category for mixed educational background as well, the sample size would have to increase to forty-five. Can you see why? To add a medium sexism category would add another row to the table with the result that the table would have 2 columns, 3 rows, and thus 6 cells. Applying our guide rule of an average of 5 per cell, we would need a sample of $6 \times 5 = 30$. If the 'mixed' category were added to the education context categories as well, the table would have 3 rows $\times$ 3 columns = 9 cells, $9 \times 5 = 45$. Make up dummy tables for each of these proposed ways of analysing the data.

For practical purposes, the sample size of student projects can be guided by two basic rules. First, 30 is the minimum sample size for most studies. Secondly, if tabular analysis is intended the sample size must be five times the number of cells in the table. Students should remember that normally much larger samples are used. By limiting both the number of variables and the number of categories used to analyse each variable, smaller samples can be used. This will provide students with worthwhile experience in the research process.

Summary

The way in which the sample studied is drawn determines the degree to which you can generalize from the findings of the study. Only randomly drawn samples ensure that the sample is representative of a larger population. While other forms of sampling are used, the findings of such studies are limited to the samples studied. Dummy tables are helpful in determining sample size, focusing the questions to be asked in the research, and preparing the way for the later analysis of the data.

Questions for review

1 Why do researchers use sampling procedures?
2 Why is it risky to rely on the observation of a single case in making generalizations about groups?

3 What are the two basic types of sampling procedure?
4 What are the advantages and disadvantages of each sampling procedure described?
5 What are the steps that must be taken in order to draw a truly random sample? Name two compromises with this ideal.
6 What are the critical issues in determining sample size?
7 While it is often necessary for researchers to study large samples in order to examine the influence of many variables in detail, what two basic rules can usefully guide the student researcher in determining sample size?
8 Read the following examples. What kind of sampling procedure was used? Why do you think the researchers chose the method they did?

a.

First year students (101) were selected randomly from three Halls of Residence and were contacted in the sixth week of the first term. In this initial study, no attempt was made to pre-select subjects according to background factors. All students were from the U.K.

The method of obtaining a sample of students for the first year group was as follows: a list of names was first extracted from a list of students obtained from the Residence Office, by means of a random number table. Two investigators visited each student (first year or post-first year) personally.

Visits usually were timed for the early evening period since at this time students were most likely to be in awaiting the evening meal. The rule operated was that if after three visits and a note, a selected student was not in or did not respond, visits were discontinued.

A comparison group of 'post-first years' comprising second, third and fourth year students, was obtained by the same process. However, as only a small percentage of post-first years remain in residence, the group contacted was small ($n = 25$). No attempt to contact post-first years out of residence was made, because it was felt desirable to control for living accommodation as far as possible.

Fisher, S., Murray, K., and Frazer, N. A., 'Homesickness, Health and Efficiency in First Year Students', *Journal of Environmental Psychology* (1985), 5, no. 2, June, pp. 181–9.

b.

The sample consisted of all children entering the reception classes from nursery classes of 33 infant schools in the

Inner London Education Authority in September 1982.
These schools came from six divisions within the ILEA
and, in keeping with the aims of the study, were in
multiracial areas. Each school, to be included, had to have
at least two children entering whose parents were white
indigenous and two children entering whose parents were
of Afro-Caribbean origin. Only schools with nursery
classes were chosen. This enabled some control over the
possible influence of nursery education on progress, and
allowed children to be individually tested just before they
left the nursery during June and July 1982. The majority
of three- and four-year-olds in the ILEA do attend some
form of nursery education.

The majority of the schools were in working-class areas,
often relatively disadvantaged. On most demographic
indices (for example the proportion of children receiving
free school meals, fathers in semi- and unskilled
occupations or unemployed) the schools were below the
mean for the ILEA as a whole.

There were 343 children in all. Not surprisingly, the
largest two groups were children whose parents were white
indigenous (n = 171) and children whose parents were Afro-
Caribbean in origin (n = 106). The Afro-Caribbean children
are henceforth referred to as the 'black' sample, but it
should be remembered that we do not include here children
whose parents are of African or Asian origin. The numbers
of children in the other ethnic groups were small and their
test results are therefore not presented. All the results
presented below refer to the black/white sample of 277.

Blatchford, P., Burke, J., Farquhar, C., Plewis, I., and
Tizard, B., 'Educational achievement in the infant school: the
influence of ethnic origin, gender and home on entry skills',
Educational Research (1985), 27, no. 1, February, pp. 52 f.

c.

In order to conduct research into this area a group of
12 teachers agreed to discuss their views on professional
values by means of a series of semi-structured interviews.
The teachers were from Catholic and Protestant schools
and they had a range of teaching experience from two
years to 26. Professional values were explored in connec-
tion with topics such as professional autonomy, teacher-
pupil relations, a teacher's freedom to pursue his or her
own methods, discipline, sources of professional identity
and the social and political backgrounds to teaching.

The interviews were conducted over a period of six months and were held either in the interviewee's school or home. They lasted, on average, for a period of one-and-a-half hours and were tape-recorded for later examination. The analysis of the interviews was aimed at extracting a series of 'domain concepts' which provided a framework for professional values and which could also be tested empirically with a larger group of teachers. Consequently, a number of statements were constructed around the themes which emerged from the interviews. These were put in questionnnaire form and sent out, by post, to a representative sample of 300 teachers throughout the province. The return rate was 73 per cent, and the questionnaire items were analysed, as a result of which 30 out of the original 70 items were rejected as being inappropriate or insufficiently discriminating. The amended questionnaire was posted to a representative sample of 910 teachers in Northern Ireland in both school systems and in all six counties. It was organized along three dimensions: pedagogic values, academic values, and social/political values.

McEwen, A., 'Teachers' values: a case study of Northern Ireland teachers' *Educational Research* (1985), 27, no. 1, February pp. 19 f.

Phase 2
Data collection

Collecting data

Words to wise researchers
The ethics of research
Attention to detail
Questions for review

By now you should be well aware that doing research involves far more than data collection. The research process does not begin, nor does it end, with data collection. Before worth-while data collection can be done the researcher must:

1 Focus the problem.
2 Identify and define the basic concepts involved.
3 Select variables that relate to each of the concepts under study.
4 Devise ways of measuring each of the variables.
5 Select a research design which will provide the desired information about the relation between variables.
6 Decide on a sampling procedure.
7 Draw the sample.

Unless each of these essential first steps is completed, data collection will often be done in a wasteful, haphazard, and unproductive way.

If preparatory steps are completed, data collection can proceed smoothly, efficiently, and with little wasted time or effort on the part of either researcher or the subjects of the research. Time is a scarce resource for most researchers. Moreover, someone who is being interviewed has the right to expect the researcher to be organized, efficient, and professional. But more about this later.

There is a sense in which, having done all the preparation, all that is required of this chapter is to say: *Go to it!* While that is true there are a few hints that are important.

Words to wise researchers

You are about to go out and collect some data. After all the time spent in preparation you are no doubt eager to get out finally and do it. Here are a few friendly tips.

First of all, be considerate. You are asking people to do you a favour. You are appealing to their generosity to help you with your work. This is true even if you are asking friends, family, or students you know. It is much more true if you are going into the community to do your research. You have a responsibility to the subjects of your research to be considerate and not to waste their time. Moreover you have a responsibility to researchers who will come after you not to irritate and alienate the community. By being inconsiderate or poorly prepared you let yourself down, waste the time and effort of others, and jeopardize future research.

Part of being considerate is being prepared. Another part is to take up only as much time as is essential. Not only does an unnecessarily long questionnaire waste your time but it also wastes the time of those to whom it is administered. Ask yourself, is this question necessary? Do I really need to know how many children the respondent has? If the study is about sharing tasks between husband and wife, then yes, you probably do want to ask that question. But if you are inquiring about past achievement in maths, you may decide to eliminate the question. Does each question really relate to the hypothesis? Or, is it really a bit of my personal curiosity? Clearly focused interviews and questionnaires not only produce better data, they are less disruptive and wasteful.

Another reason for being considerate with the subjects of your research is that what you are doing involves a certain amount of invasion of privacy. If respondents sense that you are being intrusive or asking inappropriate questions, they may refuse to co-operate, or may sabotage the research by giving misleading answers. It is often best to avoid doing research into very sensitive areas of inquiry. Leave research into such areas to those with more experience. Your manner and the nature of your research should be carefully designed so as not to offend or embarrass or annoy those you are studying. They are doing you a favour.

Part of being a considerate researcher is to be careful about the way you seek permission from those you wish to study. It is appropriate to tell people why you are doing the research. It is usually not wise to tell them what you hope to find. Many researchers now offer to tell those they studied what they found and what conclusions they drew. This often provides interesting feedback to the researcher and to those studied.

If your research involves studying people or groups outside your institution, it is often advisable to have a letter of introduction signed by someone in authority. This may help you to gain the co-operation of those you wish to interview or answer your questionnaire. It is also important for those supervising your research to have a good look at what you are planning to do. In some circumstances a letter of introduction will give you legitimacy, an acceptable reason for asking questions. It will give those being studied the sense that the researcher is accountable and is undertaking something worth while.

It is customary in all research to assure those who participate that their responses and all information collected about them will be kept confidential and that after the research is completed the questionnaires will be destroyed. It is not appropriate to have a giggle with your mates over the information you have collected. This is often a great temptation to those who are beginning to do research. If you expect people to answer questions about themselves and their families honestly and openly, the very least you can do is to keep their answers strictly confidential.

Part of maintaining the anonymity of your respondents and the groups you study involves the way you report your findings. It is often best to be vague. 'A group of students' or 'factory workers in the north of England' was studied. Sometimes fictitious names are invented. If you have to refer to individual cases in your report, fictitious names help to maintain an appropriate flow of reporting prose. Both individuals and groups have a right to privacy and to anonymity. It is your duty to protect that right.

For the most part, we recommend that students learn to do research by designing projects which can be done within an educational setting. This makes data collection much easier, since the source of the data is right at hand. It also involves less potentially disruptive use of community resources. A great deal of creative and worth-while research can be done within schools and colleges.

To sum up, when gathering data be considerate of the needs, feelings, and privacy of others. Be careful to ask permission and keep the provisions of any agreements you make with the subjects of your research. For example, if you say that you will let the subjects of your research have a copy of your results, make sure they get one. If you agree not to publish your results until you have the permission of a group or organization, stand by the agreement.

The ethics of research

Various bodies from professional associations to university councils have developed codes of ethics to guide researchers. These have been developed to ensure that an over-zealous researcher does not overstep ethical bounds in data gathering. The following extract from the British Psychological Society's guidelines on 'Ethical principles for research with human subjects' is an authoritative statement of good practice.

- Whenever possible the investigator should inform the subjects of the objectives and, eventually, the results of the investigation. Where this is not possible the investigator incurs an obligation to indicate to the subject the general nature of the knowledge achieved by such research and its potential value to people, and to outline the general values accepted by psychologists as listed in the introduction to these principles. The investigator's name, status, and employer or affiliation should be declared.
- In all circumstances investigators must consider the ethical implications and the psychological consequences for subjects of the research being carried out. Investigators must actively consider, by proper consultation, whether local cultural variations, special personality factors in the subjects, or variations in procedure from procedures reported previously may introduce unexpected problems for the subject.
- An investigator should seek the opinion of experienced and disinterested colleagues whenever the research requires or is likely to involve: (i) deception concerning the purpose of the investigation or the subject's role in it; (ii) deception concerning the basis of subject selection; (iii) psychological or physiological stress;

(iv) encroachment upon privacy. Geographical and institutional isolation of the investigating psychologist increases rather than decreases the need to seek colleagues' opinions.

• Deception of subjects, or withholding of relevant information from them, should only occur when the investigator is satisfied that the aims and objects of the research or welfare of the subjects cannot be achieved by other means. Where deception has been necessary, revelation should normally follow participation as a matter of course. Where the subject's behaviour makes it appear that revelation could be stressful, or when to reveal the objectives or the basis of subject selection would be distressing, the extent and timing of such revelation should be influenced by consideration for the subject's psychological welfare. Where deception has been substantial, the subject should be offered the option of withholding his or her data, in accordance with the principle of participation by informed consent.

• In proportion to the risks of stress or encroachment upon privacy the investigator incurs an obligation to emphasize to subjects at the outset their volunteer status and their right to withdraw, irrespective of whether or not payment or other inducement is offered, and to describe precisely the demands of the investigation.

 Wherever a situation turns out to be more stressful for an individual subject than anticipated by the investigator or than might be reasonably expected by the subject from the introduction, the investigator has an obligation to stop the investigation and consult an experienced and disinterested colleague before proceeding.

• In proportion to the risks under (i)–(iv) and to the personal nature of the information involved, the investigator incurs an obligation to treat data as confidential and to conceal identities when reporting results.

• Studies on non-volunteers, based upon observation or upon records (whether or not explicitly confidential) must respect the privacy and psychological well-being of the subjects.

• Investigators have the responsibility to maintain the highest standards of safety in procedure, equipment, and premises.

- Where research involves infants and young children as subjects, consent should be obtained from parents or from those *in loco parentis*, according to the foregoing principles. In the case of children of appropriate age, the informed consent of subjects themselves should also be obtained in advance. In research involving children caution should be exercised when discussing results of research with parents, teachers, or others *in loco parentis* since evaluative statements may carry unintended weight.
- If a subject solicits advice concerning educational, personality, or behavioural problems, extreme caution should be exercised and if the problem is serious the appropriate source of professional advice should be recommended.
- It is the investigator's responsibility to ensure that research executed by associates, employees, or students conforms in detail to the ethical decision taken in the light of the foregoing principles.
- A psychologist who believes that another psychologist or related investigator may be conducting research not in accordance with the foregoing principles has the obligation to encourage the investigator to re-evaluate the research in their light, if necessary consulting a responsible senior colleague as a source of further opinion or influence.

While these guidelines are aimed at the professional researcher in psychology, the principles are relevant to all those undertaking research with human beings. The responsible researcher is considerate, does nothing to injure, harm, or disturb the subjects of research, keeps data collected on individuals and groups confidential, accurately records information, and reports the findings of the research in a public manner.

Attention to detail

While you are collecting and recording your data it is essential to pay careful attention to detail in observation. The loss of detail in data collection may make subsequent data analysis impossible. Here are some suggestions for attending to detail in the research process.

Keep notes

A research journal is a good idea. Keep a record of the ideas you have considered. Record the decisions you make and the reasons for the decisions. It is amazing how much you forget in a short time. What decisions did you make as you narrowed the focus of your research project? What forms of the hypothesis and research question did you consider? Why did you select the one you did? Why did you select the variables you did? How did you develop the measure for your variables? What issues did you consider as you chose a sampling procedure and actually selected your sample? A few notes on these issues kept in a research journal (or log book) will be of great help when the time comes to write your report. They are also helpful to answer questions people may raise about the research.

Keep bibliography cards

Another useful tip is to keep a record of the material you have read or consulted in the course of your research. If you note the details at the time you consult the material you save yourself the effort of trying to find it again later. It is best to keep both bibliography cards and note cards. Examples follow.

Dixon, B. R., and Bouma, G. D. (1981), *Human Development and Society*, Oxford University Press, Melbourne.

Figure 8.1 A sample bibliography card for a book

The information required for a book is author(s), date, title, publisher, place of publication.

Butel, J. H., Atkinson, G. B. J., 'Secondary School Size and Costs', *Educational Studies* (1983), 9, no. 3, pp. 151–7.

Figure 8.2 A sample bibliography card for an article

The information required for an article is author(s), title, journal, date, volume number, issue number (if there is one), and pages.

Harrison, A. (1985), 'The Distribution of Personal Wealth in Britain' in G. B. J. Atkinson (ed.), *Developments in Economics*, Causeway Press, Ormskirk

Figure 8.3 A sample bibliography card for a chapter (or an article reprinted) in an edited book

The information required for a chapter in an edited book is author(s), date, title of chapter or article, name of editor(s), title of book, publisher, place of publication.

Rather than providing an example for every possible type of publication, the order of the information required will be given. In this way if you encounter a type of publication you are not sure how to handle, you can work it out for yourself. If you are still confused, ask advice, for example from a librarian. There is no single universally accepted format for referencing. This one is common in the social sciences.

1 The author(s)

The authors are listed as they appear, in the order they appear, with initials or full names as you wish. If the author is a group or organization, e.g. Department of Health and Social Security, it is listed as the author.

If the author is unknown, put 'anon' for anonymous in place of the author. If the author(s) are in fact the editors of the volume place (ed(s).) after the name(s) of the author(s).

2 The date of publication

This should be the date of the edition to which you are referring. Some people put the date of original publication in brackets after the publication date if the two dates are different.

If one author has more than one publication in a year, they are listed in order of publication to the best knowledge of the researcher in the following manner:

Author (date a) _____
Author (date b) _____

3 The title of the work cited

If a book, it is underlined. If a journal article, or chapter in a book, it may be enclosed in inverted commas.

a For journal articles, chapters in books, articles in newspapers, the title is followed by a statement of the larger source of which it is a part and the pages on which it is found. The form for an article and a chapter in an edited book is given above.

b For books, government publications, newspapers (unless it is absolutely obvious), encyclopaedia, the title is followed by the publisher and the place of publication.

The general rule is that a bibliographic reference must include all the information for someone to find the reference quickly and easily. One card is kept for each work consulted. When the time comes to do your bibliography (or list of references) you need only put your cards in alphabetical order and type (or write) them up.

Keep note cards

Note cards are useful for keeping track of ideas and information you read in the sources you consult. When the time comes to write your report you need merely consult the note card and you will have all the information you need for a proper quotation and reference. Begin a new note card for each work from which you take notes. Head the card with the name(s) of the author and the date of publication. A sample card is depicted in Figure 8.4. It helps to relocate material if both bibliography cards and note cards are kept in alphabetical order.

When taking notes, put inverted commas around direct quotations and note the page on the note card. If you are summarizing the material in your own words, do not use inverted commas, but keep track of the page(s) on which the material summarized appeared.

When it comes to writing your report, should you quote from a source you will have the information needed for a proper reference on the note card from which you will draw the quotation. One convenient form of referencing uses the following format. This referencing system is called the Harvard or scientific system. The author's name(s), the date of publication and the page are given in the body of the text. In the bibliography at the end of the report the full information is listed. A reader wishing to find out more about a reference need only consult the bibliography under the relevant name(s) and date. This reduces the clutter of unnecessary bibliographic detail.

Dixon and Bouma (1981)

p. _____ "_____

_____

_____ "

(direct quotation)

p. _____ "_____

_____

_____ "

(direct quotation)

p. _____ _____

_____

_____

(paraphrase or summary)

Figure 8.4 Sample of note card

Dixon and Bouma (1981: 42) report that:

_____

_____

_____

If a direct quotation is used the quotation is placed in inverted commas.

The following form is also used:

" _____

_____

_____

_____ " (Dixon and Bouma, 1981: 92).

The decision about which form to use depends on the preference of the writer. Long quotations are usually indented.

An alternative to the Harvard system is to number the references in the text and then to spell them out at the end of the chapter. For example the text might read 'There is considerable evidence that children's behaviour is shaped by their experiences at school (1) . . . ' and then the reference would be spelled out at the end of the chapter:

1. Rutter, M., Maugham, B., Mortimore, P., and Ouston, J. (1979), *Fifteen Thousand Hours*, Open Books, London, p. 179.

The next reference would be numbered (2) and so on. At the end of the book all the authors are listed in alphabetical order.

The choice of which system to use is largely a matter of personal preference. The Harvard system tends to break up the flow of the sentence, but it does give a quick brief reference.

Data collection sheets

Keep a separate record of the data collected for each individual or group you study. Do not place the responses of more than one person on one questionnaire. It will be impossible to disentangle the results. You need one data record for each person or group. This is required for proper cross-tabulation of the results.

To do this properly you must first ask what is the unit of analysis in your research. Is it the individual, or the class, or the group? It is quite possible for the same hypothesis to be researched at different levels of analysis. For example, in the study of the impact of amount of time spent in revision on the result of a history examination, the unit of analysis was the student. A questionnaire was filled out by each student in each class so that the researcher had a record of hours spent in revision and exam result for each student. By contrast the experimental study relating to the amount of time a class had to read material for a test of comprehension used the class as the unit of analysis. This study design is described in Chapter 6 on pp. 127–30. Classes were given different amounts of time to study the material and the average results for the classes were compared. In this case a data sheet for each class was all that was required.

Similarly in the study of student snack selection the class was used as the unit of analysis. The proportion of the selections made by the whole class of sweets, fruit, or other was the datum collected. The class received the lessons on nutritious snack selection and the results for the class were recorded. In this case one data recording sheet for each class, not each student, was necessary.

In summary, be careful as you collect your data. Be careful and considerate of those you study. Be careful to carry out your research with meticulous precision and to record your findings accurately.

Questions for review

1 What seven steps need to be taken before the researcher can collect data?
2 What are some of the ethical considerations involved in doing research?
3 What information should researchers record in their journals?
4 What information should be kept on bibliography cards for:
   a a book?
   b an article?
   c a chapter in a book?

9

Summarizing and presenting data

Categories
Tables
Graphs
Means or averages
Questions for review

You have collected your data. What do you wish to do with the stacks of questionnaires, data sheets, or completed interviews? You will have made some tentative decisions about this when you prepared dummy tables earlier. None the less, when confronted with a pile of data, new problems emerge, and further decisions will have to be made. Once data have been collected it is necessary to decide how the data are to be summarized and presented.

Since this text presupposes no knowledge of statistics, some methods of data summarization and presentation will, of necessity, not be covered. This text also assumes that the projects undertaken will be very limited in scale, so that computer analysis of data is not required. However, the logic of data summarization and presentation is the same regardless of the techniques used to do it. Moreover, there is some merit in doing a few small projects, as it were 'by hand', in order to learn the logic underlying data summarization and presentation.

To summarize and organize your data involves three steps. First, *categories* must be selected in which the raw data can be summarized. Secondly, once the categories are selected the data are *coded*, that is, they are sorted into the categories. Finally, the data are *presented* in a form which facilitates the drawing of conclusions.

Categories

While data are collected in detail, they usually cannot be reported or presented in the same level of detail. In other words, it is unlikely that you will get to report all the data that you have collected. In order to summarize and present data, tables, graphs, or charts are constructed; averages and percentages are calculated. In order to do so the data must first be categorized. We saw this earlier in the case of research into the effect time spent on studying had on academic performance. Let us presume that the data presented in Figure 9.1 were recorded on the data summary sheet suggested in Chapter 5, p. 83.

As it stands no conclusions can be readily or reliably drawn from this data summary form. No pattern emerges from a quick scan of the data. The data are still in too detailed a form. More inclusive categories are required for reporting both amount of time spent in revision and result in the examination. Once the data are in hand it is possible to determine what the extremes were and what the average was. Both of these help to construct categories.

What are the extremes:
- for amount of time spent in revision

           most   least

- for result in examination?

        highest   lowest

Scan the list and record the results.

What is the average:
- for amount of time spent in revision?
- for result in examination?

An average or the mean is calculated by totalling the measures (number of hours or result on examination) and dividing by the number of measures (in this instance students).

$$\text{Mean or average history result} = \frac{\text{Total of summation of history results}}{\text{number of students}}$$

Student name	Number of hours spent in revision		Examination result	
	Raw score	Code	Raw score	Code
1 Gail	30		98	
2 John	25		99	
3 Tim	10		50	
4 —	12		44	
5 —	20		65	
6 —	22		68	
7 —	25		80	
8 —	30		75	
9 —	30		80	
10 —	20		60	
11 —	24		65	
12 —	19		55	
13 —	18		54	
14 —	21		58	
15 —	22		60	
16 —	24		62	
17 —	28		70	
18 —	26		70	
19 —	27		65	
20 —	24		60	
21 —	18		58	
22 —	19		57	
23 —	25		68	
24 —	20		65	
25 —	21		60	
26 —	14		45	
27 —	20		35	
28 —	22		50	
29 —	26		55	
30 —	10		40	

Figure 9.1 A completed data summary form for a study of the relation between hours spent in revision and result in a history examination

Several ways of categorizing these data are now possible. The students could be classified into those who studied less than the average. Similarly, the students could be classified into those whose results were above or below the average. Other ways of classification might include separating those who passed from those who did not. The results could be separated into high pass (65–100), pass (50–64), and fail.

Once the categories are selected the data are coded. That is, the raw data are reclassified into the more inclusive categories. Let us say that you decided to use the categories 'above average' and 'below average' for both number of hours spent in revision and examination result. Go back to Figure 9.1 and codify the data. That is, after each raw score indicate the category into which it fits. For example:

	Hours in revision		Result in examination	
	Raw score	Code	Raw score	Code
1 Gail	30	AH	98	AR
2 John	25	AH	99	AR
3 Tim	10	BH	50	BR

AH = above average hours   AR = above average result
BH = below average hours   BR = below average result

In this way the raw data are codified and can be more readily analysed.

You can see that if you used different categories the coding would look different. To give yourself practice, copy out Figure 9.1 and codify the data results using high pass (65–100), pass (50–64), and fail (49 or less) as the categories. Whatever categories are used the aim is to reduce the raw data to a more manageable set of categories. The categories are decided and then the raw data are coded into those categories.

The first two steps have been done. Categories have been selected and the data codified. How are they to be presented? The hypothesis guiding this research asserts that there is a relationship between the amount of time spent in revision and the result in an examination. This means that the way in which you present your data needs to show the relationship between the two variables: time spent in revision and examination result. There are several ways to do this. These are presented in the following figures.

Tables

The first form illustrated is that of tabular presentation.

Result in history examination	Amount of time spent in revision	
	Above average	**Below average**
Above average		
Below average		

Figure 9.2 A table for presenting the data from a study of amount of time spent in revision and result in an examination

In order to arrive at the numbers to put in the table in Figure 9.2 you have to cross-tabulate your data. To cross-tabulate means to put each case (in this instance each student) where it fits in the table. To do this for our example you take each student listed on the data summary sheet in Figure 9.1 and place a tick in the appropriate cell (blank cell) of a table like that presented in Figure 9.2. The first student, Gail, was categorized as 'above average' in both variables, so place a tick mark in the upper left hand cell of the table. The second student, John, was also categorized as 'above average' in both variables, so place another tick mark in the upper left cell. Student number three, Tim, was categorized as 'below average' in both variables so place a tick mark in the lower right hand cell of the table. When all the data have been cross-tabulated in this way your preliminary table should look like Figure 9.3.

When all the data have been cross-tabulated you add up the tick marks in each and put that number in the cell. What do your results look like? Your table should look like Figure 9.4. There were 11 students who were above average both in examination result and in the amount of time they spent in revision. There were two students who were above average in result but below average in time spent in revision. There were five students who were below average in result but above

Result in history examination (dependent variable)	Amount of time spent in revision (independent variable)	
	Above	Below
Above average		
Below average		

Figure 9.3 A cross-tabulation of the data in data summary sheet presented in Figure 9.1

Examination result	Amount of time spent in revision		
	Above average	Below average	Total
Above average	11	2	13
Below average	5	12	17
Total	16	14	30

Figure 9.4 The relationship between time spent in revision and result in a history examination

average in study time. There were twelve students who were below average on both variables.

The numbers at the side and bottom of the table in Figure 9.4 are called marginal totals. They are of course the same as the totals you calculated earlier for the frequencies of each variable. These serve as useful checks to make sure your coding and cross-tabulating were done accurately. It is amazing how many errors can creep in at this stage of the research process. It took us several attempts to get Figure 9.4 correct. The marginals must add up to the total used for the construction of the table. They must also add up correctly both across the rows and down

Result in history examination	Amount of time spent in revision Number of students	
Number of students	Above average	Below average
Above average	11	2
Below average	5	12

Figure 9.5 The relationship between time spent in revision and result in a history examination

the columns. It may seem a tedious exercise but it provides a critical check on accuracy. The presentation form of the table in Figure 9.4 is depicted in Figure 9.5.

How would you interpret the table in Figure 9.5? It shows a very clear relation between the two variables. It shows that the two variables are related in such a way that the more there is of one (study time), the more there is of the other (examination result) with very few exceptions.

While interpreting Figure 9.5 is relatively straightforward as it stands, sometimes it is better to present the tabular results as percentages. There are two ways of doing this. Since each accurately reflects the data but does so in a slightly different way, the selection depends on which mode of presentation is easiest to interpret. Figure 9.6 presents the findings in Figure 9.5 as percentages of the total. In all tables giving the results as percentages it is very important to indicate the total number upon which the table is based. That is why 'n = 30' (which means the total number is thirty) is placed where it is. It is a nearly universal convention to use the lower case n to refer to the number of cases in a table or graph. Thirty is usually considered the minimum number for the use of percentages in a 2×2 table like Figure 9.6. The more cells a table has, the higher the number should be.

How you read a table depends in part on which variable is the independent and which the dependent variable. In our example, time spent in revision was the independent variable and examination result the dependent variable. Figure 9.7

Result in history examination	Amount of time spent in revision	
	Above average	**Below average**
Above average	36.6	6.7
Below average	16.7	40.0

Figure 9.6 The relationship between amount of time spent in revision and result in a history examination

Result in history examination (dependent variable)	Amount of time spent in revision (independent variable)	
	Above average	**Below average**
Above average	68.7	14.3
Below average	31.3	85.7
	100% n = 16	100% n = 14

Figure 9.7 The percentage of students spending above or below average amounts of time in revision who scored above or below average in their history examination

would be read in this way. Among those students who spent an above average amount of time in revision 68.7 per cent received above average examination results, while 41.3 per cent received below average results. By contrast, among those students who spent a less than average amount of time in revising 14.3 per cent received an above average result in the examination and 85.7 per cent received a below average result. It is therefore concluded that the amount of time spent in revision had a definite effect on the examination results of this group of history students.

When you set up a table in the form of the one shown in Figure 9.7, you show the impact of the column variable (in this instance, amount of time spent in revision) on the row variable (result in history examination). This is of course exactly what you wanted to do, because amount of time spent in revision was your independent variable and examination result the dependent variable. When you construct and interpret tables it is crucial to keep in mind which is the independent and which the dependent variable. Failure to do so can lead to some nonsensical interpretations of data.

As a general rule, if you are presenting your data in tables using percentages it is best to percentage the independent variable across the dependent variable (as in Figure 9.7). In this way you display the impact of the independent variable on the distribution of the dependent variable, which is of course what you are trying to show. Thus while tables may be percentaged in a variety of ways, the most useful is one that percentages the independent variable across the dependent variable.

If you look back over Figures 9.3 to 9.7 it should become clear that the interpretation would be the same in each of these modes of tabular presentation of the data. Tabular presentation of data is very basic and very useful. To give yourself practice at tabular analysis, take the data in Figure 9.1 and recode the exam result data into the three categories of high pass (65–100), pass (50–64), and fail (49 and less). Construct tables by cross-tabulating the data again. Present the tables numerically and as percentages of the whole, row percentages and column percentages.

There are other ways of presenting data as well. Remember data are summarized and presented in such ways as to make clear the relationships that exist among the variables under study. Other ways of summarizing and presenting data include several kinds of graphs, the scattergram, and the use of means.

Graphs

In order to prepare a graph it is necessary to perform Steps 1 (selecting categories) and 2 (coding the data) of data summarization and presentation. It is also neceessary to cross-tabulate the data in some way. Take for instance the bar graph or histogram. In a bar graph or histogram the amount of space given to each variable is proportional to that variable's portion of the sample. Figure 9.8 is a bar graph presenting the same data as Figure 9.3. Essentially, this bar graph presents the information in the top two cells of the table in Figure 9.3.

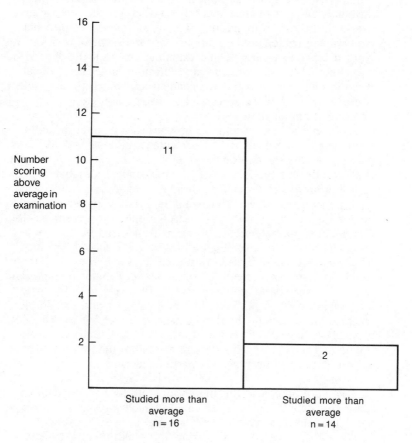

Figure 9.8 A bar graph showing the relationship between hours studied and results in a history examination

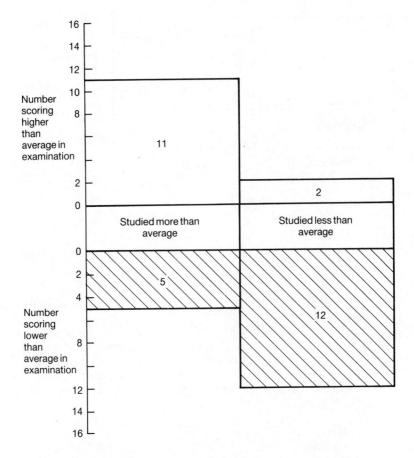

Figure 9.9 A bar graph showing the relationship between amount of time spent in revision and examination result

This is a bar graph based on the frequency distribution of the data, that is the numbers falling into each category. Figure 9.9 is a bar graph that gives all the data in Figure 9.3.

Bar graphs can also be used to present percentage data. Figure 9.10 presents the data in Figure 9.7 in the form of a bar graph. In this instance a table presented as column percentage is converted to a bar graph by making the space in the graph proportional to the percentage of each cell. The essential feature of a bar graph is that the size of the bar be proportional to the size of the variable. Again, it can be seen that different

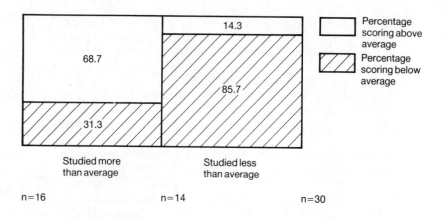

Figure 9.10 A bar graph depicting the relationship between the amount of time spent in revision and examination result

methods of presenting the same data when used correctly do not lead to different conclusions.

The pie chart is not particularly suited to the presentation of the type of data with which we have been dealing. It is much better for depicting multiple responses, or many categories or sources, when the intent is to show the proportion of each relative to the whole. For example if the ethnic composition of school was:

West Indian	2%
American	1%
Scottish	10%
English	60%
Pakistani	2%
Welsh	8%
Other	17%

A pie chart could be constructed giving each group a wedge equivalent to its proportion of the population of the school. For example, the size of the wedge to represent the West Indians must be 2 per cent of the circle's area. This can be measured by calculating what 2 per cent of 360 degrees is. There are a total of 360 degrees in a circle. Two per cent of 360 degrees is 7.2 degrees. Using a protractor, count 7.2 degrees, place a dot at 0 and at 7.2 and draw lines to the centre point of the circle, and

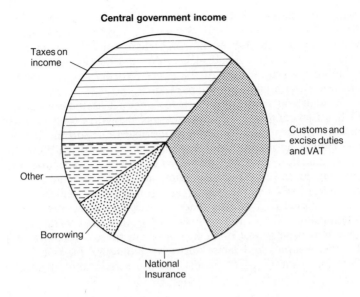

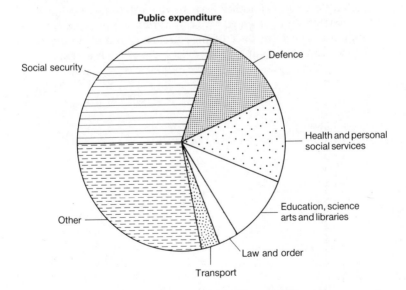

Figure 9.11 Examples of Pie Charts

you have a wedge of the pie equal to 2 per cent of the circle. Repeat this for each group. The next group, the Americans, would require 3.6 degrees. Starting where you left off (at 7.2 degrees) count off 3.6 and place a dot at 10.8 degrees and draw a line to the centre point of the circle. Working by guess will not do in the preparation of pie charts.

Pie charts are in general hard to construct accurately and very difficult to compare. For these reasons they are not usually used in scientific reporting but only in journalistic reporting, like newspapers and magazines. Annual budgets are often presented in pie charts. Figure 9.11 gives two examples of pie charts, one showing central government income and the other public expenditure. Unless the numerical information on which a pie chart is based is given, the reader must guess at the precise relationships. Thus the first chart shows that the central government gets most of its income from three sources, taxes on income, customs and excise duties (including VAT), and National Insurance. The details cannot be ascertained from the chart.

Scattergrams

The scattergram is another way in which data can be summarized and presented. A scattergram is produced by pinpointing each instance of measurement on a grid defined by the two axes of a graph. Figure 9.12 shows such a grid.

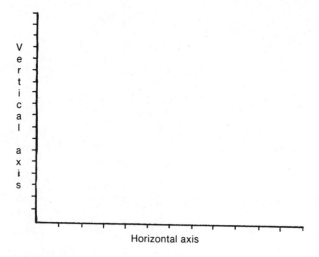

Figure 9.12 A scattergram grid showing horizontal and vertical axes

The two lines along which the units are marked are called axes and the space between them is defined by the grid formed by the intersecting lines drawn from each unit point along the two axes. The first step in constructing a scattergram is to decide on the scale of units to be used on each axis.

Data are not usually categorized and coded before constructing a scattergram. Instead the scale of each axis is adjusted so as to accommodate the range of the variable being analysed. Remember where we suggested that you do the analysis of the data from the study of the impact of amount of time spent in revision on examination result? We asked you to identify the range of each variable by noting the extremes. This is a very important step if you wish to construct a scattergram. Re-examine the data presented in Figure 9.1:

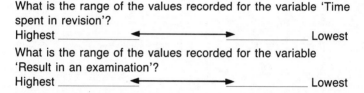

The scale of the units along each axis of the grid upon which you will produce the scattergram must be able to cope with the range of each variable. In this instance the scale of the horizontal axis, the one used to indicate hours spent in revision, must range from 10 (the lowest reported) to 30 (the highest reported). The range for the vertical axis, the axis dealing with examination result, must go from 35 to 99. Figure 9.13 presents a grid upon which a scattergram for the data presented in Figure 9.1 could be constructed. The scattergram is constructed by putting a dot on the grid in the place defined by the two pieces of data for each student. The use of graph paper makes this task much easier.

The axes are drawn and units marked along them. Now a dot is placed on the grid for each student. Student number 1 studied 30 hours and received a 98: place a dot at the intersection of a line drawn up from the 30 position on the horizontal axis with a line across from the 98 position on the vertical axis. The positions of students 1 to 5 are drawn in as examples.

Using a sheet of graph paper, make a scattergram of all the data in Figure 9.1. Normally the intersecting lines are not drawn on the table. Rather, two rulers are used to indicate where the lines intersect and only the dot is placed on the grid. Place two

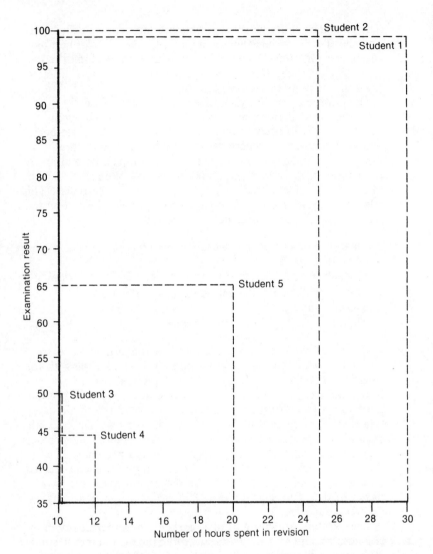

Figure 9.13 A grid for the construction of a scattergram for data on impact of amount of time spent in revision on examination result

dots close together where two data points are the same. The result is a pattern of dots. What does the pattern of thirty dots tell you?

Line graphs

A line graph shows the relation between two variables by connecting the data points on a grid defined by two axes with a line beginning at the left and moving to the right. Figure 9.15 is an example of a line graph. The data are taken from a study by Kathryn Walker. She studied the time spent in raising a child. The data were originally presented as in Figure 9.14.

Age of child	Number of hours increased
less than one year	5.2
1st year	4.6
2nd–5th year	4.0
5th–11th year	4.5
12th–17th year	3.6

Figure 9.14 Increased number of hours spent on household activities by non-employed persons due to presence of child. Data from Walker, E., and Woods, M. E. (1976), *Time Use: A Measure of Household Production of Family Goods and Services*, Centre for the Family of the American Home Economics Association, Washington, DC, pp. 50-1.

These data could also be presented by a line graph. Figure 9.15 presents the same data in line graph form. A time variable is often placed on the horizontal axis. The number of hours increased is put along the vertical axis. The units are clearly marked along each axis. Then the data points are put in place as for a scattergram. The data points are joined by a line beginning with the first dot on the left and moving to the next dot to the right.

As an exercise, convert your scattergram of the data on the relationship between number of hours spent in revision and examination result. To do so start with the dot on the far left and move to the next dot on the right. If you do this you will produce a fairly wiggly graph. You will also encounter a problem. What do you do when there is more than one dot in a vertical line? Which is the 'next dot to the right'? In such a case the average is calculated and the data point put at the average position. For example, you will begin with a problem in the data in your scattergram when you find that there are two data points in the vertical line above 10 hours in revision. One

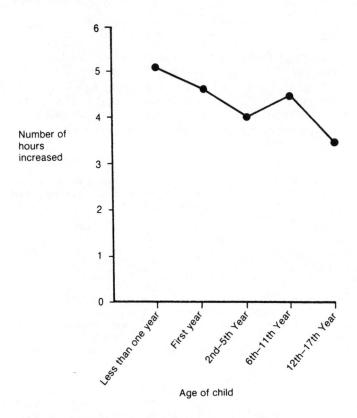

Figure 9.15 A line graph depicting increased number of hours spent on housework due to presence of child at different ages

received a result of 50, the other a result of 40. The data point for a line graph would be placed at 45. In this way a line graph smooths out some of the detail of a scattergram. It makes the pattern clearer, but it eliminates some of the variation.

There are several critical points to remember in constructing line graphs. First, the units of measure must be clearly specified, labelled, and marked on each axis of the graph. If a time dimension is in years, say so and label the units along the axis. In Figure 9.15 the vertical axis is marked off in hours (0 to 6) and labelled, 'Numbers of hours increased'. In Figure 9.16 the vertical axes are in millions of pounds on the left and 100,000s of pounds on the right and labelled as 'Growth in profits' for each company.

A second thing to watch is the use of different units of measurement for different lines. Some graphs have two vertical axes each using a different unit of measurement. While there are legitimate uses of this device, it can be very misleading. Figure 9.16 gives an obvious example of this. The graph in Figure 9.16 makes it look as though Company B is growing at a much faster rate than Company A. But is it? Read the graph carefully. Large units are used to record the growth in annual profit of Company A. Its profits grew by more than a million pounds in each five-year period, nearly doubling the amount it grew over the period of time. Small units are used to record the growth in annual profits of Company B. While the line makes it look like a real winner, its annual growth in profit is much less than Company A's. B's annual growth in 1975 is 900,000 while Company A grew by 1,800,000. The use of different units on right and left axes must be done with great care not to mislead and in general should be avoided.

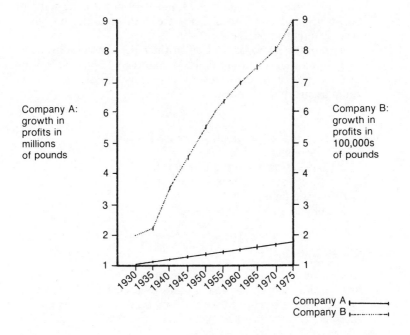

Figure 9.16 A misleading line graph using different units on two vertical axes to compare growth in corporate profits

The scale of units selected is very important to graph construction. Figure 9.16 shows that by using large units change is under-emphasized. On the other hand, using small units emphasizes the magnitude of change. Let us examine another example of this. There has been a lot of talk in recent years about rising divorce rates. The data on divorce rates in England and Wales are presented in tabular form in Figure 9.17.

Year ending	1951	1961	1971	1981
Rate	2.6	2.1	6.0	11.9

Figure 9.17 Persons divorcing per thousand married people
Social Trends

When the data in Figure 9.17 are presented graphically many things can happen. Figures 9.18 and 9.19 present the same data, but in very different ways. They are both accurate, but give very different impressions.

Despite the need for caution in their use, line graphs are a useful way of presenting data. As Figures 9.20 and 9.21 show, they can give a vivid impression of trends and also enable quick comparisons to be made.

To construct a line graph you must:
1 Select categories for your data.
2 Code the data into the categories.
3 Select a scale of units for each axis.
4 Plot the data points.
5 Link the data points with lines.

Means or averages

Means, or averages, are often used to compare groups. Means are a useful way to summarize and present data. The average performance of groups may be compared, or the average rates of consumption, or the average incidence of a particular event.

To calculate an average, or mean, one adds up all the individual data and divides by the number of individuals. For

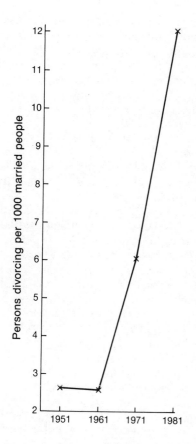

Figure 9.18 Divorce rates rising at a tremendous rate

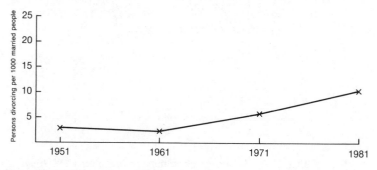

Figure 9.19 Divorce rates show little change

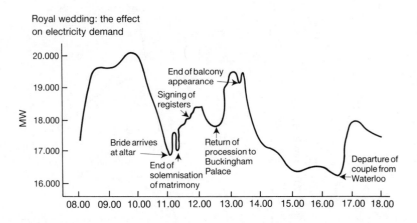

Royal wedding: the effect on electricity demand

Figure 9.20 Use of a line graph to make a point *Financial Times* 31 July 1981

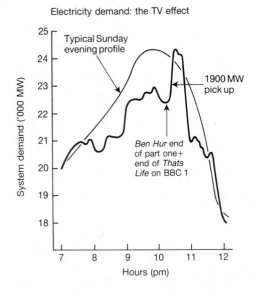

Electricity demand: the TV effect

Figure 9.21 Use of a line graph to make a comparison *Financial Times* 7 April 1981

example, you have already calculated the average number of
hours spent in study and the average examination result earlier
in this chapter.

Means could be used to summarize and present the data
from our study of the impact of the number of hours spent
in revision on examination results. The class could be divided
into two groups, those who studied more than the average
and those who studied less than the average. Once this is
done the average examination result for each group could
be calculated. First divide the students into two groups.
Remember, the average time spent in revision was 21.7
hours.

Group A Studied more than average		Group B Studied less than average	
Student	Mark	Student	Mark
1	98	3	50
2	99	4	44
6	68	5	65
7	80	10	60
8	75	12	55
9	80	13	54
11	65	14	58
15	60	21	58
16	62	22	57
17	70	24	65
18	70	25	60
19	65	26	45
20	60	27	35
23	68	30	40
28	50		
29	55		
16	1125	14	746
Group A average = 1125 ÷ 16 = 70.3		Group B average = 746 ÷ 14 = 53.3	

Figure 9.22 The calculation of mean test scores for two groups of
students

The data in Figure 9.22 would simply be reported in this way. The group of students who studied more than the average received an average result of 70.3 while the group of students who studied less than the average received an average result of 53.3.

As an exercise, calculate the average number of hours spent in revision for each of two groups of students. First do it for those who received above average results and then do it for those who received less than average results.

We saw that the move from a scattergram to a line graph involved the loss of a certain level of detail in the presentation of the data. When groups are compared using means, all variation internal to each group is lost.

Scattergram	Presents most information
Line graph, or bar graph, or pie chart	Presents less information
Mean or average	Presents least information

A further disadvantage of the mean is that it may conceal considerable variations. If the owner of a small business said that the average income of the five workers in his employ was £100 a week, this might seem reasonable. However, if the actual wages were £50, £50, £50, £50, plus £300 for his son the manager, the figure for the average would give a misleading impression. This disadvantage can be overcome by calculating the standard deviation, which gives a measure of the spread of the data. The method used to calculate the standard deviation can be found in statistics books.

One advantage of the mean compared to graphs is that it allows precise mathematical comparisons to be made. Moreover we are often interested in group performance and not so interested in the outstanding cases. The average is a useful indication of a characteristic of a group. Trends in averages, like trends in percentages, are particularly useful. The Central Electricity Generating Board, in predicting energy supply requirements for the month of January, will rely on trends in average energy consumption for the last twenty Januarys. It will not be interested in the variations in individual household consumption.

Summary

Once your data are collected they are ready to be summarized and presented. To do this requires that you select categories in which to summarize your data. While you did some preliminary thinking on this when you constructed your dummy tables, the final selection is done when your data are in hand. Once you have selected categories the data are coded into the categories. Then the data are cross-tabulated in some way to show the relationship between the variables in question. We have looked at tables, graphs, and means as the basic techniques for summarizing and presenting your data.

Questions for review

1 What are the three steps involved in summarizing and organizing your data?
2 Why is it necessary to categorize your data?
3 What are the advantages of Figure 9.6 over Figures 9.5 and 9.7?
4 What does it mean to cross-tabulate your data?
5 Describe the difficulties associated with your graphs.
6 What is a scattergram?
7 What are the advantages of using means or averages versus line graphs versus scattergrams in presenting data?

Phase 3
Analysis and interpretation

10

Drawing conclusions

What did you ask?
What did you find?
What exactly do you conclude?
To whom do your conclusions apply?
Questions for review

You have now reached the point where you analyse and interpret the findings of your research. You have clarified your thinking, formed a hypothesis and gathered data. Now what? Essentially it is time to draw conclusions about your hypothesis on the basis of the evidence you have collected.

A proper conclusion is grounded on a careful analysis and interpretation of the data gathered in the light of the basic question being researched. Data have been collected and presented, but they still require evaluation and analysis. Four basic questions guide the activities of data analysis and interpretation:

1 What did you ask?
2 What did you find?
3 What do you conclude?
4 To whom do your conclusions apply?

What did you ask?

The first step in drawing conclusions is to remember what it was you asked. It is surprising how easy it is to lose sight of the purpose of a piece of research. Before leaping to conclusions, it is useful to remind yourself of the questions which originally motivated you to do the research. You may have made many interesting discoveries as you gathered data or prepared your data for presentation. But what was the central issue?

Do you remember the questions that you first asked? If you kept a research journal you should look back to remind yourself of your original questions. Some of the original questions will seem very broad and unfocused now. You may be able to see how, in the process of clarifying your thinking and narrowing the focus of the research, you essentially tackled a manageable part of a much larger issue. Try to clarify now how you see both the larger issue and how the research you did relates to that larger issue.

The clearest statement of what you are asking is your hypothesis or your research objective. Recall the process by which you narrowed the focus of your project and formed the hypothesis or objective. Now look at your hypothesis again. How does your hypothesis relate to the larger issues? Take as examples the hypotheses we have used in this book.

We have spent a lot of time on research involving hours spent in study and exam results. The hypothesis stated:

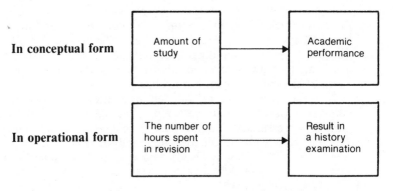

What was the background of this hypothesis? According to Chapter 3, p. 30, it had been observed that some students get better marks than others. This prompted a series of clarifying questions. Refer back to Chapter 3 to remind yourself of the other possible explanations that were put forward. It should become clear that your hypothesis and hence your research will tell you something about the general issue; but not all. There were other factors which were not explored. Hence any conclusions you draw will be limited to the factor you examined. Your research pertains to the general area but deals specifically with one isolated factor. When asked, 'Why do some students get better marks than others?', you cannot conclude, 'Because some study more than do others.' You know there are many possible factors. Your research deals with only one. You could conclude that 'amount of time spent in revision seems to be a factor in examination results.' Your research dealt with one aspect of the overall issue. Be careful to ensure that in drawing a conclusion you draw attention to the general issue and the way your research relates to it.

The first step in drawing a conclusion is to re-state the general issue and the hypothesis showing how the hypothesis relates to the general issue.

Another hypothesis used as an example through this text concerned the relationship between lessons on 'nutritious snack selection' and the selections students actually made in the tuckshop. Re-read the sections of Chapter 6 in which this example is first developed. Then answer these questions.

1 What is the general area of concern?
2 What was the conceptual hypothesis?
3 What was the operational form of the hypothesis?
4 How does the hypothesis relate to the general area of concern?

Here again you can see the importance of stating conclusions in such a way that they are clearly related both to the specific hypothesis and to the general issue. There are many ways in which the nutritional status of high school students could be studied. In this case snack selection in the tuckshop was taken as the area. First a general observation study was done to discover what the patterns of selection were. Then an experiment was conducted to ascertain whether a teaching unit on nutritious snack selection would change students' snack selection patterns. The conclusions of such research would relate to the general areas of student nutrition, tuckshop operation, and nutrition education. How does the specific hypothesis tested relate to each of these areas? In this way the conclusions of a small study are related to larger issues.

The first step in drawing conclusions is to clarify the way the research you have done relates both to the hypothesis and to the larger issue. You did not start measuring and weighing babies for no reason at all. What were the reasons? How does what you did relate to these reasons? If you did research comparing the degree of sexism among different groups of boys, why did you do so? To conclude simply that levels of sexism among boys who had attended co-educational schools were higher or lower or the same as those among boys who had attended single-sex schools may be correct but too limited.

Relate the findings of your small study to the larger context of which it is a part.

What did you find?

Once you have reminded yourself what it was you were asking and how your hypothesis or research objective related to that general area of interest, you can ask 'What did I find?' Yes, the data your study produced are by now displayed in tables or graphs or expressed as averages. But what do you think they say? They do not analyse or interpret themselves.

There are several basic aspects to answering the question 'What did you find?' First the data need to be interpreted. Then data are related to the hypothesis or research objective. Thirdly, you need to evaluate the data. We will discuss each of these aspects.

First, what do your data, as presented, say? This involves ·. expressing in words what the tables, graphs or averages say. We spent some time on this in Chapter 9. Look again at Figure 9.7. It is followed by a simple statement expressing in words the relation between the data in the table. That is an example of interpretation.

Now turn to Figure 9.8. What does it 'say'? The interpretation of this graph might be written in this way:

Among those 16 students who studied more than the average amount of time, 11 (or 68.8%) received an above-average result in the history examination while among those 14 students who studied less than the average amount of time, 2 (or 14.3%) received an above-average result.

To interpret your data means to re-state the relationships depicted in your tables, graphs, or average as clearly as possible in words.

How would you interpret the data presented in Figure 9.11 regarding central government income and public expenditure? The interpretation of data depends partly on the question asked. Let us assume that the question was:

What are the main items of public expenditure?

In this case the interpretation is relatively easy, because a pie chart can only convey a limited amount of information. The interpretation might be:

The largest expenditure is on social security. Defence, health, and education are the next largest items and are roughly the same size. Other items are relatively small.

As an exercise, try your hand at interpreting the data presented in Figure 9.15. Remember, to interpret the data means to re-state in words the relationship between the variables presented in the table, graph, or average. Finally, interpret the data presented in Figure 9.17.

Once you have interpreted the data you are ready to relate the findings to the hypothesis or research objective. That is, what do these data tell you about your hypothesis? Is the evidence for or against the hypothesis? What are the implications of the findings for the narrowly defined research question?

This is usually fairly straightforward. Problems emerge if the data are unclear, when there is no strong trend one way or the other. If this should be the case, the analysis should state that the implications of the data for the question in hand, or the hypothesis, are unclear.

Again, it is best at this stage to report the implications of the data without discussion or comment. Either the hypothesis is supported or it is not. Ambiguous findings cannot be taken as support. It is important to remember that a hypothesis is never proven to be absolutely correct. Rather a hypothesis is tentatively accepted, or likely to be correct given the evidence, or it is not accepted given the lack of evidence.

Once the findings are stated and related to the hypothesis or research objective it is time to evaluate the data and to acknowledge the limitations of the study. General issues are critical here. First, the operationalization of the variables would doubtless have left you not entirely satisfied. Again, if you kept a research journal, you would have noted limitations in it. These limitations can be noted at this point in the report or earlier in the discussion of variable selection, decisions regarding research design, sample selection, and data collection. You may have questions about the instrument (questionnaire) or the interviewers. The limitations of your sample are to be noted.

The most important limitations have to do with the possible influence of those variables you were unable to control or to measure. These possible alternative explanations for the relationship between the independent and dependent variables need to be noted. You may have suggestions for future research. It may be that your findings were not clear, and you suspect the interference of some variable. It is useful to note this.

Your findings may have come out in an unexpected fashion. It is here that you can comment on this and suggest explanations. Your findings may conflict with the findings of others. This can be discussed.

Whatever they are, acknowledge the limitations of the study. This shows that you know what might have been done if you had more time, or money, or other resources. It also shows that you know your conclusions are made *tentatively* in the knowledge of the limitations of your research.

What exactly do you conclude?

A good conclusion has two levels. First it states clearly and simply exactly what the data reveal. Secondly, it relates this simple statement to the larger issues. This can be seen to be the reverse of the process by which you narrowed your attention in the first stage of the research process.

Here is a sample conclusion for the study of revision time and marks:

Conclusion

A study of 30 students in a history class in a state school in _____, revealed that those who spent more than the average time in revision tended to receive above average results in a history exam. While there were some exceptions, the data as presented in Figure 9.5 show a clear trend in this direction. It is safe to conclude that these data provide evidence that supports the hypothesis.

Thus it is likely that amount of time spent on revision is one among other factors which affect academic performance. Other factors such as IQ, social life, nutritional status, and specific study habits may account for some of the exceptions in this study. Further research is required to establish how widely this finding holds. Further research should compare other students at other schools; the effect of time spent in studying on the examination results in other subjects, and on the results of other methods of examination.

A conclusion like this states the highly specific conclusion based on the data collected, summarized and presented. It then moves to the general issue stating the implication of the data for the larger issue and suggestions for future research. The first part of the conclusion re-states what the data reveal about the operational form of the hypothesis. Do the data support the hypothesis? Do they reject the hypothesis? Or is the situation unclear? Then the implications of the acceptance or rejection or lack of clarity of the hypothesis are drawn for the conceptual form of the hypothesis and finally for the larger issue. Data do not speak for themselves. The role of a conclusion is to re-state the findings of the study and to draw the implications of the findings for both the hypothesis and the larger issue.

Take the example of the study comparing sexist attitudes among boys. The hypothesis (see Chapter 5, p. 85) stated that:

> Boys who have gone to single-sex schools are more sexist in their attitudes towards women than boys who have attended co-educational schools.

The dummy table suggested for this study is found in Chapter 7, Figure 7.8. Let us assume that Figure 10.1 presents the data from a study of 60 boys in the first year in two suburban secondary schools.

Sexism score	Educational context	
	Single-sex school	Co-educational school
high	24 (80%)	20 (67%)
low	6 (20%)	10 (33%)
total	30 (100%)	30 (100%)

Figure 10.1 Findings from a hypothetical study of sexism among boys

Sexism score	Educational context	
	Single-sex school	Co-educational school
high	14	5
moderate	10	10
low	6	15
	30	30

Figure 10.2 Findings from another hypothetical study of sexist attitudes among boys in two educational contexts

Given the data in Figure 10.1 what would you conclude about your hypothesis? Is it supported or rejected, or, are the results unclear? The data in Figure 10.1 do not present an immediately clear picture. They are not compelling. There is too little difference. A conclusion drawn from a study such as this based on these data might read as follows:

Conclusion

In an attempt to determine whether educational context played a role in the development of sexist attitudes among secondary school boys, a sexist attitude questionnaire was administered to two groups of secondary school boys. One group had attended single-sex schools for all of their schooling, the other group had attended co-educational schools. Does an educational context in which boys regularly have to interact with girls produce lower levels of sexist attitudes?

The results of our research indicate that boys from both educational contexts show high levels of sexist attitudes as measured by the sexist attitude scale used in the study. Boys from single-sex schools are slightly more likely to have highly sexist attitudes. The differences between these two groups of boys is not sufficiently large to conclude that the hypothesis is clearly supported. While the data are in the hypothesized direction, the relationship is too weak to draw any firm conclusions.

While educational context may well have an effect on the development of sexist attitudes among boys, it cannot be concluded that this is so on the basis of this research. Additional research is required to ascertain whether this relationship is stronger or weaker in other schools. It may well be that the general level of sexism in our society is such that educational context has little effect on the development of sexist attitudes among teenage boys.

Again, the role of the conclusion can be seen. It relates the specific findings back to the hypothesis and then to the general issue.

As an exercise, write a conclusion for this research given the findings in Figure 10.2.

In writing your conclusion be sure to:

1 Re-state the general aim of the research.
2 Re-state the finding of the research.
3 Indicate whether the hypothesis is supported or rejected, or if the result is unclear.

4 Explain the implications for the larger issue.
5 Make suggestions for future research.

In the conclusion you state what the data as summarized and presented in your tables, graphs, or averages, tell you about the hypothesis you formulated. The implications are then drawn for the larger issue. This is also true for a research objective. However, research objectives are not accepted or rejected. The data are simply summarized verbally and a conclusion drawn.

Take the example of the simple observation study of one baby's growth. Once the data have been collected and recorded, the simplest conclusion would be that the baby had grown by the addition of __ cm and __ g. But there was a background to this study. You could look up the average growth rates for infants and compare this baby's growth record with that standard. Then a conclusion about one baby's growth in comparison with the average could be made.

Since no specific comparisons were being made, nor were data on other factors kept, no other conclusions could be drawn. If the purpose of the study had been to compare the growth rates of different infants, let us say one group that had been breast-fed and another that had been bottle-fed, then the study would have had a hypothesis about which conclusions could be drawn.

An appropriate conclusion for a study of infant growth guided by a research objective might take the following form.

Conclusion

The purpose of this study was to observe the growth of one infant over a period of eight weeks in order to see, in a specific infant, the general patterns of growth as described in the textbooks. The specific measures were of growth in length and weight. Other aspects of growth and development were observed but not systematically recorded.

The baby I observed grew by __ cm and __ g during the eight-week period of observation. The baby was eight weeks old at the beginning and sixteen weeks old at the end. A growth of __ cm and __ g is well within the bounds of normal growth for infants of this age.

This observation has also made me aware of the complexity of observing infant growth and development. I would suggest that in future observations of this type the following be considered . . .

While a conclusion about a hypothesis is not drawn, the conclusion of a study guided by a research objective may well make suggestions for future research. For example take an observation study guided by the following research objective:

> To discover what factors are considered by the person(s) in charge of meal planning in the selection and preparation of food.

The researcher might conclude at the end of the research as follows:

Conclusion

An observation study conducted in ten households revealed the following factors to be taken into consideration in the selection and preparation of food:

- cost
- availability
- preparation time required
- nutritional quality
- balance and diversity in foods
- calorie content of foods
- preferences of family members

  While in this household cost was the predominant factor, closely followed by preference of family members, this may well vary from household to household. Future research into the factors shaping household decision-making about food should ascertain how the importance of these factors varies among households.

  While we interviewed each member of the household, we discovered that in this household one person is responsible for meal planning and preparation. Given our experience in this household we suspect that this person is not always 'The Mother'. This means that future research can focus on one member of each household, but that care is required in selecting which member to interview. We also suspect that a questionnaire could be devised to measure the relative importance of various factors . . .

The researcher here used the observations of a single case study as the basis for many suggestions for the next round of research on this issue. She could well have made other comments.

Further observations regarding the amount of time spent in meal preparation, meal planning, and shopping, might have been made as well. The researcher might also have commented on the accuracy of the information available to the person who was observed and the suitability of the meals planned to the purposes outlined by the person.

Thus, whilst research guided by a research objective does not lead to conclusions about hypotheses, the results are summarized and related to the general issues behind the research. Suggestions for future research may also be made.

So far we have carefully avoided discussing more mathematical forms of analysis and there is not space here to discuss the application of statistical analysis to data, but the conclusions that you can draw by using non-statistical techniques are often very limited. In recent years a number of programs have been written which allow quite complex analyses to be made by students who consider themselves to be weak in mathematics. If computer facilities are available, and your data is suitable for statistical analysis, it is well worth while seeking advice on the use of appropriate programs.

There are a number of books available which introduce statistical methods to social scientists, and you may wish to consult one of these. They include:

Levin, J., (1977) *Elementary Statistics in Social Research*, 2nd edn, New York, Harper & Row

Marston, P., (1982) *Applied Business Statistics*, London, Holt Rhinehart

Maxwell, A. E., (1978) *Basic Statistics for Medical and Social Science Students*, London, Chapman and Hall

To whom do your conclusions apply?

The question 'To whom do your conclusions apply?' can be answered in a narrow sense and in a broader sense. On the one hand, your conclusions are limited to the sample studied and to the population of which it is representative. This is the narrow interpretation of a conclusion.

If you studied a representative sample of history students in a particular school, your conclusions are limited to history students in that school. If you observed one family, your conclusions will be applicable only to that family. If you studied two classes of home economics students, your conclusions are limited to those students.

This narrow interpretation of the applicability of conclusions is based on the limitations imposed by the sampling procedure selected. This narrow interpretation refers to the data, to the 'facts' produced by the research. Take the example of the study of sexist attitudes among secondary school boys. The data in Figure 10.1 relate to two groups of 30 boys. Each group had a different educational background. The specific findings are limited to those boys. That is, the finding that two-thirds (67 per cent) of boys from co-educational schools scored high on sexist attitude, while four-fifths (80 per cent) of boys from single-sex schools did so, is limited to those boys. If those boys were a representative sample of a larger population, then that finding applies to that larger population. It is not permissible to conclude that, in general, 67 per cent of boys from co-educational backgrounds will score high and 80 per cent of boys from single-sex schools will score high.

The conclusions regarding the data apply to those from whom the data were collected, or to the larger population of which they are a representative sample.

On the other hand, research is done to gain some understanding about larger issues. Some of the conclusions drawn refer to the implications of the findings of the research for these larger issues. This is the broader sense of the applicability of the conclusion. In drawing conclusions, the researcher moves from the narrow conclusions about the findings of the study to the implications of those findings for the larger issues. It is in this sense that conclusions have a broader applicability.

Again, take the example of the study of sexist attitudes among secondary school boys. The data in Figure 10.1 were interpreted too closely to conclude that educational context made much difference between these two groups of boys. Then the conclusion moved on to discuss the implications of the findings for the larger issue. When drawing the implications, a much more tentative style of expression is adopted: 'It may well be that . . . ', 'Although additional research is required . . .'

The sample conclusion for a study of thirty history students demonstrates the shift between the narrow conclusion and the drawing of implications. First it summarizes the empirical findings, the data, then it continues, 'Thus it is likely that amount of time spent in study is one, among others, of the factors . . . '

Thus in drawing conclusions, the first step is to re-state the empirical finding. This part of the conclusion applies narrowly and strictly to those studied or the population of which they are a representative sample. Then the implications of the empirical findings for the more general issues are discussed. In this the findings are related to a broader context and made more generally relevant. However, the discussion of implications is done tentatively. In this way the conclusion can be seen to have a narrow aspect, the summary statement of the empirical findings, and a broader aspect, the discussion of the implications of these findings.

Questions for review

1 What four basic questions guide the activities of data analysis and interpretation?
2 Interpret in words the data in this graph. Note that your task is simply to re-state in words what is presented in the graph. Do not try to explain or moralize or draw conclusions.

Average amount of weight loss of returning patients at various intervals

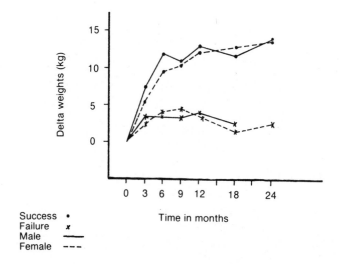

Source: *Food and Nutrition Notes and Reviews*, Vol. 37, no. 2, April–June, 1980, p. 63.

3 Why is it important to acknowledge the limitations of a study?

4 How does the sampling procedure you chose influence the conclusion you can draw?

11

Writing up your research

Before writing
Hints on style
Format
After you have finished writing

By now you have focused on a research issue, identified and measured variables, drawn samples, selected research designs, collected data, summarized and presented the data, drawn conclusions and discussed implications. You are now ready to write the research report. If you have kept a research journal you will probably have a mountain of notes and records. These will be very valuable to you in writing the report.

We have not said anything about the research report until this time because it is the last activity in one cycle of the research process. The process does not begin with how to write a report. The research process consists of a series of activities which are undertaken and then reported. Not everything that is done during the research is reported in the research report. The research report summarizes the activities in such a way that they are clear to the reader and so that the reader could repeat the research. *Replicability* is a characteristic of good research.

Before writing

There is a great temptation to rush into writing because this gives a feeling of something accomplished, and indeed it is true that certain sections of the report can sometimes be written in draft form before the research is complete. In general, however, it is better to spend time clarifying your ideas and deciding precisely what it is that you want to write before you actually put pen to paper in a formal way. Instead you should jot down ideas, talk about them with your friends, work out a plan, and talk about what you intend to do with your supervisor.

Again, before starting to write it is essential to check any regulations. Are any limits laid down for the length of the report? If so, get some idea of how many pages this represents and make a rough allocation of words (or pages) to each section of your report. In some cases there may also be regulations about style and layout, the form which references must take and so on. It is far better to find these out in advance and conform as you go along rather than make hasty adjustments at the end.

Check what time you have available. Writing up a research report can be a time-consuming business, so you should draw up a timetable, making sure that you leave adequate time for re-writing, typing, and then checking and correcting the typing. Typists are usually helpful, but it is only fair to give them adequate time to do a proper job. It is a useful precaution to sound out a typist, giving some indication of length and the time you expect to hand over the manuscript. You can also discuss charges.

There are a number of books which give useful suggestions on writing up research, such as:

Berry, Ralph, (1966), *How to write a research paper*, Oxford, Pergamon
Turabian, Kate L., (1973), *A manual for writers of term papers, theses and dissertations*, Chicago, University of Chicago Press

Hints on style

Style depends on purpose. A news report in the *Sun* will be written in quite a different way to a Ph.D. thesis. In the case of a research report you need to vary the style and presentation according to whether the report is intended to convey information for general use, specific information for participants in an event, as in a discussion paper, or as a formal requirement for a course. The language you adopt will vary according to the purpose. A research report which is to be assessed is a formal document and the language and style should therefore be appropriate.

Remember to give references whenever these are needed — these help to make replication possible. Don't plagiarize; if you make use of other people's words or ideas you should make appropriate acknowledgement. Divide up the report, for example by using the format below. It is often useful to number the sections so that you can refer back to a specific point. Diagrams and charts can help to make the presentation clear and attractive.

Format

The format will vary according to the type of research you have undertaken. The headings below are meant as a guide, and you may decide to omit some of them or to amalgamate when this seems appropriate.

Title page

This should give the full title, your name and possibly your address, and also the date.

Acknowledgements

A number of people will probably have helped in the research and it is proper for you to acknowledge this. It is conventional to thank your supervisor, particularly if he or she will be assessing it! Thank your typist and also those such as headteachers who have given you permission to use their facilities.

Abstract

This may not be required; if so you are lucky, because it can be quite difficult to condense a long report into relatively few words. A useful technique is to ask and then answer relevant questions such as

What was the aim of the research?
How did you go about it?
What were the results?

Introduction — statement of the problem

This is your starting-point. You should say why you undertook the research — what the problem is and why it is important.

Review of the literature

Depending on the particular piece of research, the review of the literature may not appear as a separate section, but instead be incorporated as you go along so that appropriate literature is surveyed when a new section of the report is introduced.

However, it is usual to undertake a formal review of the literature early in a research report. A good review is not a kind of photocopy of earlier writers, but makes use of *relevant* reading to develop an argument. It should link back to the statement of the problem. If previous writers had answered the problem which you are investigating there would be no need for your research. Consequently your review will show what is known already and how your research will fill a gap in knowledge or replicate earlier work. The review must use a proper referencing system as shown in Chapter 8. Make sure that you do this as you go along, otherwise you will complete the first draft and then have to spend long hours in the library checking publishers or page numbers.

Research design

The description of the design of your research will depend on the particular project you have undertaken. However, it is possible here to pick out a line of argument which will apply to many reports. A good way to start is to explain your hypothesis or research objective and how any variables were selected and operationalized. If the research involved choosing a sample you need to explain carefully how this was selected and how it relates to the population as a whole. A table or chart often helps.

The next step is to outline the test material, questionnaire, or experiment. This needs to be an explanation and justification of your methods. If there are inadequacies in what you have done, point them out. All research has limitations and it is presumptuous to pretend that yours is perfect.

A good way to write this section is to do it chronologically, explaining what you have done and why. For example, you will describe any piloting before you go on to the main part of the research.

Data description

Describe your findings. This can often be done briefly, perhaps by making use of tables or charts as described in Chapter 9. All these need to be numbered and given a title.

Data analysis

This is the section where you interpret the results of the research. You need to be cautious, particularly if your sample was small. Use your tables as evidence to substantiate your analysis.

Conclusion and implications

A useful way to organize your conclusion is to begin by referring back to the introduction where you stated the problem and also to the hypothesis. To what extent have you illuminated the problem? You must identify the shortcomings in your research. This makes it easier to evaluate your work. If your research has been inconclusive, say so; in many cases nil results are valuable, and in any case readers may be as interested in your methods as in the results.

Point out the implications of your findings for policy or for other researchers and show what further research needs to be done.

Bibliography

This should include all the books and articles you have read which are relevant to the research, and these should be presented in alphabetical order. It should not include those you ought to have read but haven't.

Give your references in a proper form.

Appendices

These should be numbered and given a title. Material put in appendices is often that which would spoil the flow of the argument if incorporated in the text, for example copies of questionnaires and raw scores on tests.

After you have finished writing

One difference between a good research report and a poor one is the time and trouble taken after the first draft is complete. Finding out can be intellectually exciting; checking is usually tedious.

You need to read through what you have written checking spelling, punctuation, grammar, and references. Then go through again checking the argument. Where is this weak? Have you claimed more than the evidence supports? It is often useful to get a friend or colleague to read through what you have written and to make constructive suggestions.

When you are sure that you cannot improve the report, hand it over to the typist. Give clear instructions about layout, e.g. size of margins, spacing. Give the typist enough time to do a good job; then check carefully to ensure that there are no typing mistakes. You will probably also discover some mistakes made by you. Ask the typist to correct these as well.

Appendix

A table of random numbers

To use this table of random numbers it is necessary to pick a starting-place. One way of doing this is to ask someone to pick a number between 1 and 32 in order to select a column in which to start and then to pick a number between 1 and 50 to select a row.

Once a starting-point is selected it is permissible to move in any direction (up, down, to one side, or diagonally) so long as the movement is systematic.

Let us assume that the task is to select a sample of 30 from a population of 90. The elements (persons, tests, laboratory animals, or whatever) in the population would be numbered from 1 to 90. The task is to select randomly 30 of the 90 numbers. Let us assume that your starting-point was row 19 column 30. Since you are selecting two-digit numbers it makes the most sense to use the numbers in column 30–31. Hence the first number is 06. If you choose to move down the column the second number to be selected is 41. When you reach the bottom of the column start at the top of columns 28 and 29 and work down until you have selected 30 numbers. This will comprise a random sample of 30 from a population of 90.

row																COLUMN NUMBER																		row
	1	2	3	4	5	6	7	8	9	10	11	12	13	14	15	16	17	18	19	20	21	22	23	24	25	26	27	28	29	30	31	32	
1	2	7	8	9	4	0	7	2	3	2	5	4	2	6	7	1	6	8	5	9	1	3	5	4	0	3	6	6	7	6	5	1	1
2	2	2	6	0	4	1	7	7	3	8	7	3	6	7	9	4	2	1	3	8	9	0	3	4	9	0	2	6	3	0	9	8	2
3	9	1	6	6	3	9	4	9	1	0	5	1	5	2	2	7	5	2	5	3	4	1	3	9	5	8	1	3	8	2	9	2	3
4	7	0	5	5	9	2	7	5	7	8	0	8	8	5	0	6	0	5	9	0	5	7	4	5	2	0	6	1	6	4	2	0	4
5	1	7	3	6	6	3	9	8	2	1	7	9	7	6	4	2	4	9	6	0	3	6	3	5	3	9	9	1	8	5	1	3	5
6	8	2	0	2	8	7	7	6	0	2	2	3	1	1	1	6	4	8	5	2	2	3	4	2	2	6	5	2	2	4	9	6	6
7	0	8	7	5	3	3	6	4	2	6	8	3	1	6	5	0	0	5	5	7	8	1	0	1	2	9	1	4	3	4	7	6	7
8	9	4	1	9	0	8	4	6	6	8	6	3	3	2	2	3	7	4	7	5	1	5	7	6	3	7	9	4	5	5	3	5	8
9	5	0	0	6	7	4	0	0	0	1	9	5	9	9	1	8	1	4	7	4	9	8	7	2	4	3	0	8	6	4	2	7	9
10	1	9	5	1	1	5	2	6	2	9	4	1	1	5	8	4	4	4	6	1	8	7	8	6	4	8	7	4	4	0	5	8	10
11	5	6	4	4	1	8	7	2	8	3	6	1	5	9	8	6	2	2	9	1	9	0	4	8	1	0	1	3	5	3	4	4	11
12	7	9	2	5	1	9	7	9	3	1	8	6	8	7	7	6	6	5	0	3	8	1	1	2	4	7	8	9	1	7	5	2	12
13	3	3	3	5	9	5	1	4	0	8	2	5	6	3	5	4	6	5	7	2	6	7	8	9	9	9	8	0	9	1	5	3	13
14	1	9	0	1	0	0	9	9	5	7	4	1	5	9	4	7	6	4	8	2	6	4	4	1	8	8	1	5	4	3	8	0	14
15	5	4	4	7	2	0	3	7	9	1	0	9	6	2	9	7	4	7	6	1	1	6	1	2	2	9	5	8	4	4	8	6	15
16	2	9	8	2	5	5	9	3	2	0	4	9	0	6	4	4	2	1	5	7	3	6	5	5	4	5	7	9	6	6	4	0	16
17	9	7	6	2	6	7	7	7	3	3	3	1	7	5	0	9	6	1	1	3	9	2	1	1	0	0	1	3	7	7	3	7	17
18	5	8	2	4	3	3	0	8	5	3	5	7	5	8	3	5	9	3	4	5	4	6	3	9	2	7	1	1	4	9	1	3	18
19	4	3	4	9	5	0	3	6	2	9	7	4	6	2	5	6	9	8	3	6	1	4	0	3	5	9	7	1	8	0	6	9	19
20	1	1	9	3	4	8	0	6	7	0	9	7	9	6	9	9	4	0	6	0	0	5	9	6	5	1	4	2	0	4	1	9	20
21	6	9	1	8	3	3	7	5	9	6	6	7	7	6	0	4	5	3	4	5	7	3	0	6	1	0	3	0	0	3	5	0	21
22	7	0	0	3	8	1	3	4	7	9	5	2	6	9	9	7	3	2	5	0	2	3	5	3	9	7	4	8	9	4	1	5	22
23	3	7	2	0	8	1	5	6	9	0	1	7	8	9	6	6	6	0	7	8	1	9	6	7	4	8	9	6	3	6	5	1	23
24	2	7	0	0	0	6	5	0	6	5	6	0	3	2	9	3	1	7	2	2	8	4	9	0	4	3	2	4	5	5	1	2	24
25	3	0	7	0	7	8	4	9	4	2	8	2	4	7	4	9	6	0	4	5	8	1	7	7	0	9	8	4	6	3	1	2	25
26	6	2	9	3	3	1	7	7	5	2	2	3	4	6	4	2	2	4	7	5	4	4	4	1	7	1	6	7	1	2	6	8	26
27	5	4	9	2	1	4	8	5	7	0	9	6	4	7	2	1	8	9	7	6	1	3	3	4	6	6	5	9	0	7	0	3	27
28	0	3	7	0	1	7	3	8	0	3	6	2	3	1	0	9	5	5	2	5	9	2	0	2	8	7	7	2	0	2	7	2	28
29	9	3	6	6	2	2	0	9	7	2	3	9	2	8	7	3	1	0	7	0	8	9	3	8	8	5	3	1	3	1	0	9	29
30	2	9	5	6	9	9	5	6	9	8	2	8	0	0	4	4	8	8	5	7	2	1	3	4	9	5	2	6	8	3	6	6	30
31	8	5	7	2	9	2	6	5	9	3	9	7	1	8	3	5	6	6	1	2	1	5	5	6	1	7	1	5	7	5	9	7	31
32	8	4	5	7	7	9	9	5	1	4	5	5	0	9	5	3	1	3	9	3	7	8	1	4	0	5	4	1	5	4	4	0	32
33	8	7	9	8	1	8	4	1	4	3	7	7	0	9	1	9	4	6	1	3	8	6	5	9	2	2	8	1	6	9	0	1	33
34	7	3	2	5	1	8	6	3	2	8	5	8	6	9	3	4	5	2	6	1	9	0	6	9	0	5	4	6	8	0	3	2	34
35	8	9	9	0	1	8	8	8	9	5	7	5	0	4	1	1	6	0	3	1	3	0	3	5	8	9	2	7	8	8	7	1	35
36	0	2	9	7	8	8	1	7	6	1	6	7	6	4	2	5	0	5	8	3	2	4	7	7	2	2	6	2	6	8	6	0	36
37	0	5	2	3	2	3	8	1	8	8	1	6	2	3	0	7	3	0	1	2	6	2	6	8	3	7	4	4	3	8	9	9	37
38	2	2	6	8	1	6	9	6	2	6	7	9	1	7	8	0	2	4	8	0	4	7	3	3	8	4	4	8	4	3	3	8	38
39	0	7	8	4	9	5	8	8	0	7	2	1	8	1	7	5	3	0	7	4	1	0	3	2	0	1	2	8	6	5	9	4	39
40	4	8	0	7	0	5	9	9	4	9	6	9	8	2	0	6	4	0	7	8	1	1	4	2	1	6	7	0	7	3	1	2	40
41	9	2	0	1	6	7	2	8	3	9	8	8	3	4	7	8	4	0	5	1	6	8	7	8	3	5	4	5	0	4	0	6	41
42	0	8	8	3	4	0	9	2	2	8	1	5	0	4	8	3	2	6	2	9	2	1	9	8	5	3	1	0	7	8	5	3	42
43	2	0	6	9	7	5	2	8	2	5	5	4	0	7	7	1	7	8	6	8	5	1	3	7	8	2	7	1	9	3	6	3	43
44	3	1	8	6	8	3	5	6	3	2	7	4	1	8	9	4	5	6	8	0	6	4	6	4	1	0	9	1	9	8	1	4	44
45	0	0	8	6	1	7	5	0	8	5	6	5	0	8	2	7	1	1	6	3	4	6	0	9	4	7	9	2	4	8	7	0	45
46	3	3	2	9	4	2	5	3	3	8	2	4	2	6	2	5	2	9	0	1	3	7	6	5	9	1	4	6	0	1	0	0	46
47	8	4	7	4	0	4	5	1	2	1	0	4	2	5	7	7	9	4	6	5	8	3	3	3	1	0	3	7	7	7	8	6	47
48	0	2	4	3	0	2	0	7	2	8	8	0	8	4	1	6	0	2	3	5	9	7	5	1	3	6	3	2	8	7	5	8	48
49	4	6	5	6	3	0	4	5	2	0	1	5	2	7	9	5	3	0	2	2	1	6	1	1	0	0	9	1	6	1	7	7	49
50	3	4	8	3	4	5	8	7	5	9	7	1	6	3	9	9	0	9	4	2	5	8	9	5	3	3	3	6	4	5	2	0	50

Index